Small Business, Banks, and SBA Loan Guarantees

Small Business, Banks, and SBA Loan Guarantees

Subsidizing the Weak or Bridging a Credit Gap?

Elisabeth Holmes Rhyne

QUORUM BOOKS

New York • Westport, Connecticut • London

Library of Congress Cataloging-in-Publication Data

Rhyne, Elisabeth.
    Small business, banks, and SBA loan guarantees : subsidizing the
weak or bridging a credit gap? / Elisabeth Holmes Rhyne.
        p. cm.
    Bibliography: p.
    Includes index.
    ISBN 0–89930–256–4 (lib. bdg. : alk. paper)
    1. Small business—United States—Finance. 2. Loans—United
States—Government guaranty. 3. United States. Small Business
Administration. I. Title.
HG4061.R48 1988
338.6'42'0973—dc 19   87–36098

British Library Cataloguing in Publication Data is available.

Library of Congress Catalog Card Number: 87–36098
ISBN: 0–89930–256–4

First published in 1988 by Quorum Books

Greenwood Press, Inc.
88 Post Road West, Westport, Connecticut 06881

Printed in the United States of America

∞™

The paper used in this book complies with the
Permanent Paper Standard issued by the National
Information Standards Organization (Z39.48–1984).

10 9 8 7 6 5 4 3 2 1

Contents

Figures

Tables

Acknowledgments

I wish to thank three institutions and several individuals for helping to make this study possible. First, I am grateful to the Small Business Administration (SBA), for making their loan history data available to me on computer tape, through the director of the Office of Planning and Budget, Lawrence Rosenbaum. Second, the Congressional Budget Office helped arrange for me to use the SBA data and provided financial support. In particular, I would like to thank Richard Emery for the enthusiasm and generosity with which he assisted in making the arrangements. Several members of the computer systems section of the Budget Analysis Division, under Robert Harris, very cooperatively performed the necessary translation of the data into a form my personal computer could digest. Third, I am indebted to the Brookings Institution for use of their facilities, particularly their computer, and for financial support. At Brookings, I would like to thank Barry Bosworth for many discussions about government credit programs which have helped clarify my thinking, and Robert H. Meyer, for help with statistical work at a crucial point.

Helen Ladd, John D. Montgomery, and Jim Coates provided comments that have significantly contributed to making this a better evaluation. My greatest debt is to Herman B. Leonard, who has given me valuable technical, procedural, and conceptual assistance, and has been a source of cheer and encouragement throughout the study's progress.

The material in this book is adapted from my doctoral dissertation for the Kennedy School of Government, Harvard University, entitled "An Evaluation of the Small Business Administration's Business Loan Guarantee Program" (September, 1985). A condensation of the main line of argument appeared in Chapter 5 of *The Economics of Federal Credit Programs*, Barry Bosworth, Andrew S. Carron, and Elisabeth H. Rhyne, published by the Brookings Institution (Washington: 1987).

Introduction

The Small Business Administration's (SBA's) business loan guarantee program is an attempt by the federal government to increase the access of small businesses to credit and in so doing to stimulate growth in the small business sector. Not all agree that the program succeeds. Here are two representative views.

This loan guarantee program is a vital source of long term capital for this country's small business community. It is a program which generates revenues in excess of its costs to the government and is an excellent partnership between the public and private sectors.[1]

Unfortunately, neither stated SBA policies nor empirical analysis of SBA's lending patterns provide any evidence that subsidized SBA credit assistance serves *any focussed or rigorously defined public policy purpose at all*. . . . Rather than serving a *public good, these programs may inflict unfair private economic harm*: the 99% of unsubsidized small businesses (i.e., non–SBA borrowers) in the sectors where SBA lending is concentrated undoubtedly face downward pressure on market shares, prices, profits and return on investment owing to the artificial presence of government fostered and subsidized competitors.[2] (emphasis in original)

The first statement was made by the head of the National Association of Government Guaranteed Lenders, a group of banks that make SBA-guaranteed loans, formed to lobby for the program's continuation. The second statement came from David Stockman, who as Director of the Office of Management and Budget was probably the program's most vehement and effective critic during the 1980s. Neither are dispassionate observers.

Although their statements are typical of the debate on the program, neither reflects a serious analysis of how well the program works or what effects it produces. The claims that the program generates revenues in excess of costs and that SBA harms competing nonassisted businesses cannot be empirically documented, and the remaining claims are in large part matters of opinion. Impartial analyses, based on empirical results, are almost completely lacking in the three and a half decade history of the loan guarantee program. This book attempts to help fill the gap in knowledge about how well the program works and to apply that knowledge in a comprehensive examination of the major public policy questions surrounding the program.

THE PROGRAM

Under the 7(a) business loan guarantee program, the SBA offers to guarantee loans made to eligible businesses by commercial banks and certain other lenders.[3] Until 1986, the guarantee usually covered 90 percent of principal and all interest, though for loans of over $100,000 the coverage was permitted to fall to 70 percent (but very rarely did). In 1986, the 90 percent guarantee was made mandatory for loans up to $155,000, while larger loans were given a range of 70 to 85 percent. The terms of the guarantee stipulate that whenever a borrower is over 60 days in arrears either the lender or SBA can call the guarantee into effect. On demand, SBA purchases the guaranteed portion of the loan's currently outstanding principal and unpaid interest. Thereafter, SBA owns the loan and has first responsibility for collection.

Any business that meets SBA's definition of small, which differs from industry to industry, may be eligible for an SBA guaranteed loan. Firms in a few selected industries, including banking, real estate development, and publishing, are not eligible. The main further qualification is that banks must certify that the business would not qualify for credit on reasonable terms without the guarantee and that prospects for repayment are sound. The loans range in size to an upper limit of $500,000 (guaranteed portion). The average size in 1984 was $167,000 (full principal; average guaranteed portion was $145,000).[4]

The program concentrates on the intermediate range of maturities. The majority of loans carry maturities of five, seven, or ten years. They are usually used for a combination of working capital and fixed asset purchases, with emphasis on the latter. Interest rates of up to 2.25 percent above the current prime rate are permitted, or 2.75 percent above for loans of over seven year maturity. The rates actually charged average somewhat below the ceiling, and are comparable to rates on nonguaranteed small business loans. All loans are secured by tangible assets of the companies and, if need be, owners. They are fully amortized through equal monthly payments.

Banks play a crucial role in the program. They have primary responsibility for choosing the firms to receive guaranteed loans and usually initiate the involvement of SBA. When faced with loan applications they consider appropriate, banks submit guarantee applications which SBA must approve. These contain information on the financial standing of the firms and their credit worthiness. About two-thirds of all banks participate as lenders, though only a much smaller proportion have active programs. In variations of the basic program, some banks are given promise of a three day loan approval time by SBA (certified lender program), a select group obtains permission to make loans with no prior SBA approval (preferred lender program), and all banks are allowed to sell the guaranteed portion of the loans into a secondary market.

In 1986, SBA guaranteed 16,800 loans, totalling approximately $2.8 billion.

THE NEED FOR EVALUATION

The SBA program goes on and on, operating from year to year with relatively little change. Its duration, three and a half decades, is not inconsequential, and neither are the program's effects. During this time it has played a quiet but steady role in the lives of two major types of U.S. institutions, small businesses and banks, at the expense of a third, the federal government. It has affected hundreds of thousands of businesses, at the rate, during the 1970s and 1980s, of between 15,000 and 20,000 per year. As the businesses receive credit they might otherwise have not obtained, the effect has usually come at critical points in their life cycles. SBA's clients represent a cross section of U.S. businesses, particularly the retail, wholesale, services, and manufacturing sectors. They range from sole proprietorships to companies employing 50 to 100 workers. A disproportionate number of the borrowers are new companies and minority-owned businesses.

The loan guarantee program has also become a fixture in the commercial banking community. Although only about 1 percent of all business credit receives the guarantee, the program is a significant force in the context of its market niche: intermediate term business loans below $500,000. One source estimates that as much as 42 percent of small business credit over five years in duration is guaranteed by SBA.[5] Most banks participate at least minimally in the program, and many banks use SBA guarantees as an active part of their business strategies.

These are the visible aspects of the SBA program. It has another, less visible side. Its services are provided at a cost to U.S. taxpayers. Each year the expected subsidy value of the credit SBA guarantees is 11 percent of total new loans.[6] In 1986 this amounted to $286 million. This is not a hidden interest rate subsidy, but the expected amount of cash SBA requires to administer the program and pay for defaulting loans. While this is not a major drain on the federal budget, it is enough, when paid year after year, to warrant careful scrutiny.

The SBA program's longevity, size, and impact are sufficient reasons for a thorough evaluation. But there are other reasons as well. One of these is the central role of the program within the SBA. Business loans have traditionally been the heart of the SBA. They were the primary reason for the agency's creation in 1953, and today the guarantee program reaches the largest number of businesses, with the largest amount of loan dollars of any of SBA's activities. While the years have seen a gradual increase in the importance for SBA of other programs (disaster loans, small and minority contract procurement, advocacy, SBICs, MESBICs, etc.), the basic structure of SBA's organization still revolves around business loan guarantees as the core activity of its branch network. SBA's identity remains closely tied to the guaranteed loans.

A broader motivation for the study is to explore the efficacy of government credit programs generally, using SBA as an archetype. The government uses loans and loan guarantees for a variety of purposes, but many share the same problems and pitfalls. SBA's experience can give insight into the problems that other programs may encounter and that could be expected in any new attempt by the government to enter credit markets, especially business credit markets. In particular, credit programs face a common and difficult interplay between their political and economic goals and performance standards. How these forces interact in SBA's case is a central concern of this book.

Finally, the loan guarantee program is a part of U.S. industrial policy. It is one of a few federal attempts to induce business growth directly, through a program, rather than through policies in areas such as tax, regulation, trade, or economic stabilization. A direct programmatic approach involves the provision of assistance to individual businesses. While such programs have been rare on the federal level, they have proliferated at the state and local level, and are used in many countries both developed and developing (some with U.S. government assistance). Proposals are made from time to time for the federal government to start new direct economic development programs as one weapon in the attempt to improve American productivity and competitiveness. Not all the direct programs or proposals involve loan guarantees, but many involve the provision or subsidization of term finance. The SBA program can serve as one example, and an example with adequate experience, of how well the government can administer a direct economic development program and how effective or ineffective direct intervention through credit can be.

Despite the size and age of the SBA program and despite its potential broader implications, it has been evaluated surprisingly little. There have been few full-scale evaluations of the program. Studies by Timothy Bates and by Richard Klein have revealed some information on financial performance, based on aggregate data, and have made useful observations about problems and needed reforms.[7] The General Accounting Office (GAO) has performed studies of specific aspects of the program, using information collected in field visits and surveys. In 1976 GAO studied loan management, and in 1983 it studied the certified lender and secondary market programs. From within SBA, the former chief actuary, J. R. Estefania, performed the most thorough analysis of individual loan data to date and produced long-run default rates and subsidy estimates. He used data from SBA's Loan Accounting System, which is also the main data source used here. Unfortunately, SBA did not publish his results, which included data up to 1978. While each of these analyses is useful and has been helpful in the preparation of this study, all are limited in some respect. An evaluation is needed that both takes a comprehensive view of the program and brings to bear extensive data on the program's experience.

The program received some scrutiny as a result of a general concern with reforming the budget treatment of government credit programs. This focused largely on including budget controls on both the annual volume of lending and the subsidy. While improving budgeting is important, one of the motivations for this evaluation is to show that the biggest challenges in dealing with the program are internal. The tasks are to improve management and to insure that the program produces benefits that justify the subsidy afforded to it.

The lack of evaluation can best be attributed to the needs and attitudes of the political supporters of SBA and of economists. Throughout most of its lifespan the loan guarantee program has enjoyed widespread, bipartisan support. While the support may have been somewhat shallow, it did not need to be strong because concerted opposition was not raised against it. This has allowed the program to evolve slowly, without commanding great public attention. The program was shaken by Reagan administration budget reduction advocates who each year recommended phasing out or significantly shrinking the program. Despite the program's more vulnerable position, however, the attention to evaluation of program performance did not increase greatly.

On the other hand, the widespread perception that the program primarily serves political and ideological needs has been another reason for the relative lack of scrutiny. Economists seem to have yielded up the program to politicians, regarding it as outside their sphere of interest. There is some validity in this attitude. The program can accurately be seen as a way of meeting certain desires of the small business and banking communities and giving politicians a chance to affirm their commitment to the ideal of American entrepreneurship.

Yet, such an attitude misses an important point. Even if the underlying motivations for continuing it are political, the SBA program has definite effects on finance and the economy. It alters the pattern of credit allocation and subsidizes selected businesses. Moreover, whatever their underlying motivations may be, program advocates use language to justify the program that is either overtly economic or subject to testing by economic standards. The program is said to overcome structural problems in credit markets that prevent full service to small businesses and to reach a segment of all businesses that is particularly productive of social and economic benefits. These claims deserve to be tested, and if they are found to be lacking, either the program or its claims to continuation must change. This study was performed in the belief that the fruits of economic and financial analysis can and should be an important element in the political decision-making process.

AREAS OF INVESTIGATION

There may be little research on the program, but there is no lack of unresolved issues concerning program performance. Several important questions surface repeatedly. This study examines three groupings of issues: first, default and subsidy costs; second, the role of banks; and third, the program's ultimate social and economic goals.

One might expect that two of the most important questions concerning the performance of the loan guarantee program would be: what is the rate of default among borrowers, and what should the rate be? Neither has been sufficiently addressed. Attention has been diverted from the loan guarantee program by significantly higher defaults among other SBA programs, such as the economic opportunity and direct business loan programs. By comparison, the loan guarantee program has performed well. There has been no clear standard from which to judge an appropriate rate, and most of those involved with the program have been content with the published figures. This inattention is also partially a reaction to the published figures on defaults. These have generally understated the rate of default, as they are not given in the most relevant form. One cannot discern the proportion of borrowers who fail from regularly available information on the status of the portfolio. Consequently, this key question rarely enters debate.

The default rate is closely related to another important measure, the amount of subsidy paid by the government. Because guaranteed loan interest rates are close to market levels on similar nonguaranteed loans, the program is often regarded as unsubsidized. However, default costs borne by the government and not covered by guarantee fees constitute a subsidy to the borrowing group as a whole. Again, open questions are what the subsidy is and whether it is an appropriate amount. Without answers to these questions, debate remains poorly informed.

A second set of issues concerns the role of banks as the day-to-day administrators of the program. Here the question receiving most attention is whether the program offers a fair return to banks. Some critics of the program argue that the guarantee gives banks a chance to earn excess profits. On the other hand, banks often complain that the program is too costly and cumbersome to provide an adequate return for their participation. Unlike the default and subsidy questions, the question of bank profitability occupies a central place in arguments for and against the program, but again, this question has been insufficiently examined.

An equally important approach to viewing the role of banks follows from the observation that banks should carry out the responsibilities delegated to them in a way that furthers the effectiveness of the program. First, this means that they should use SBA guarantees to extend credit to borrowers they would not ordinarily serve and on loan terms beyond ordinary practice. Second, they should not contribute unnecessarily to a high level of defaults. Knowledge about how banks respond to the incentives the program sets out for them can lead to consideration of ways incentives could be changed to improve the program.

Finally, the ultimate purposes of the program remain at issue. The program can be viewed as emerging from a set of political and ideological forces including bank and small business interest groups, the special place of small business in public conceptions of American capitalism, and the needs of Congressional representatives to respond to these. But political motivations are not the same as public goals. Those who speak and write publicly about the program emphasize broad social goals including overcoming disadvantages small businesses face in credit markets and promoting businesses likely to create rapid employment growth. In program operations some of the aims are pursued more actively than others. This study concludes that the program does not maximize its potential social and economic contributions.

These three sets of issues, default and subsidy costs, the role of banks, and the program's ultimate purposes, are the central concerns of this evaluation. To draw conclusions about each of these, a detailed empirical description of how the program worked during the decade from 1973 through 1983 was constructed. This consists of models of the timing and incidence of default among SBA loans and of the financial impact of the loans on the banks that make them and on SBA itself. These models form a foundation for understanding actual program experience that is far more detailed than most ordinarily available information.

Building on this understanding, it is possible to assess how well the program has performed. One portion of that assessment takes the perspective of management efficiency, and asks whether the program fulfills its appointed functions at the least possible cost. The other portion looks to the ultimate social goals of the program. Finally, specific recommendations are offered on how the program can be improved.

At the conclusion of the investigation a picture emerges of a program that is not as efficient or as socially and economically productive as it could or should be. Defaults, which affect nearly one borrower in four, are excessive, and require SBA to pay for guarantee claims in amounts equivalent to 9 percent per loan, plus 2 percent for program administration. This default rate is not a necessary result of lending to SBA's desired target group. Rather, it is greatly influenced by bank decision making. Because the guarantee percentage has been so high, averaging 87 percent during the decade studied, banks have been all but absolved of the need to select borrowers carefully. It is found that banks do not make an excess profit on SBA loans, but that they tolerate a number of defaults among SBA loans that is ten times as large as the number they tolerate in their regular portfolios. Program efficiency would be greatly improved by SBA's use of a guarantee percentage low enough to give banks a meaningful stake in the outcome of the loan, probably between 65 and 80 percent.

With respect to the program's ultimate goals, SBA administers its program, particularly during the 1980s, as if it were pursuing the goal of overcoming a credit market gap: it involves itself little with borrower selection, placing ever more responsibility into bank hands. It clearly has an impact on bank lending patterns, inducing them to make longer term loans and to serve new borrowers. Yet SBA allows the default rate subsidy to continue, and this undermines the credit market correction image of the program. A subsidized program must show that its beneficiaries are worthy of the subsidy. SBA can show that a small portion of its borrowers come from minority and other disadvantaged groups, but for the 85 percent that are not in such a group, SBA is at a loss. No evidence is available to show that these borrowers, who look very much like a cross section of ordinary small businesses, are particularly productive of benefits such as rapid growth, job creation, innovation, or promotion of competition. Nor does SBA make any attempt to identify high-productivity borrowers.

SBA has improved the program during the 1980s, largely by the introduction of the certified and preferred lender programs that bring the program closer into line with its credit market perfecting image. But the persistence of defaults remains a stumbling block. This book recommends that through a combination of (1) expanding certified and preferred lenders, (2) reducing guarantee coverage, and (3) raising guarantee fees, SBA move to streamline operations while reducing defaults. It suggests that SBA is ready, at this point in its long history, to embrace the standard of financial self-sufficiency, and thereby to focus on becoming a genuine credit market perfecting program.

Returning for a moment to the two views quoted above, the results of this analysis show that both are partially right. The program is indeed a strategic source of long-term capital. However, its public-private partnership, that is, the SBA-bank relationship, is so lax that it allows banks to select businesses that are too likely to default. If it tightened this relationship, SBA could induce banks to supply term capital to a stronger portion of the small business community. Stockman's claim that the businesses who do not receive SBA assistance are harmed by the program has not been substantiated through empirical techniques, and the use of such techniques would probably yield inconclusive results. However, he is right that SBA's recipient patterns demonstrate a scattershot approach to the small business sector, and that SBA should make a greater effort to aim its activities towards specific public goals.

ORGANIZATION OF THE BOOK

The analysis of the loan guarantee program begins with a brief history of the SBA program and its predecessor in the Reconstruction Finance Corporation. The first chapter also describes the program's political environment, including the nature and intensity of interest group support. One purpose of this chapter is to provide background on why the program takes its current shape. The chapter also introduces themes that will be important throughout the analysis. In particular, it shows the central role of banks in the program. Bank limitations are the main program justifications, and bank wishes are the main influences on specific program policies.

Chapter 2 begins the analysis of the program's financial performance. It focuses on the timing of default and repayment of loans, and on the final disposition of loans SBA has purchased. The goal of this section is to determine the long range rates of failure, first the number of loans that go into default and second, the number that are finally declared unrecoverable. These are found to be 23.5 percent and 19.5 percent, respectively. The chapter also describes how defaults are related to economic conditions.

The third chapter assesses the impact of SBA loans on banks. It is based on a model of the cashflows to and from banks holding portfolios of SBA loans. The major question addressed in this section is whether banks make a competitive return for their participation. When the result suggests that returns are barely adequate, the remainder of the chapter investigates possible motivations for bank participation, strategies banks adopt to increase returns, and types of banks that use the program.

The fourth chapter determines the cost of the program to the SBA, the long-run subsidy. It then compares the returns banks make in varying circumstances to those of SBA, in light of the fact that bank decisions determine SBA costs. It finds that current loan guarantee agreements give banks few incentives to guard against excessive defaults.

The analysis turns in Chapter 5 to the social goals of the SBA program. The finding is that the program clearly does not fulfill one of its main objectives, the correction of a flaw harmful to small businesses in financial markets. Though no final judgment is reached on the other main objective, inducing borrowers to produce social and economic benefits, it is observed that the program is not well structured to pursue that end.

Chapter 6 describes the changes that SBA has made in the program during the 1980s, the certified and preferred lender programs, and the secondary market. These are all changes that improve the management efficiency of the program and bring it closer to its goal of correcting a credit market flaw.

Chapter 7 lays out possible policy changes that could improve management efficiency and fulfillment of social goals. It offers recommendations for reform ranging from minor management improvements to major program restructuring.

The problems of SBA are not unique. This analysis illustrates issues relevant to government credit programs in general. For example, most encounter difficulties in evaluating long-run costs. They struggle to determine whether their relationship to private financial institutions is appropriate, and they have difficulty estimating the real economic impact of their assistance. This study develops a framework for analyzing these problems as they apply to the SBA program. Chapter 8 sketches how that framework could be applied to other major credit programs.

NOTES

1. Brooks H. Brown, vice-president, Allied Lending Corporation, quoted in U.S. Congress, House Committee on Small Business, *Summary of Activities*, 99th Cong., 2nd sess., January 1987, H. Rept. 99–1036, p. 344.

2. David Stockman, director, Office of Management and Budget, quoted in U.S. Congress, House Committee on Small Business, *Financial Assistance Program Termination*, Hearings, 99th Cong., 2nd sess., 1986, pp. 153–54.

3. The 7(a) refers to the section of the Small Business Act that contains the program's authorization, which may be found in 15 USC 636(a).

4. Small Business Administration, "Management Information Survey," internal document, October 1984, p. agencywide 1.

5. U.S. Congress, General Accounting Office, *SBA's 7(a) Loan Guarantee Program: An Assessment of its Role in the Financial Market*, GAO/RCED–83–96, April 1983.

6. Author's estimate, developed in Chapter 4.

7. Timothy Bates, "A review of the Small Business Administration's Major Loan Programs." (Washington, DC: Interagency Task Force on Small Business Finance, December 1981); Timothy Bates and William Bradford, *Financing Black Economic Development*. (New York: Academic Press, 1979); Richard Klein, "SBA's Business Loan Programs," *Atlanta Economic Review*, No. 28 (September-October 1978): pp. 28–37; and Richard Klein, "Financial Results of the Small Business Administration's Business Loan Portfolio," *University of Michigan Business Review* (January 1978).

1 Historical and Political Context

The histories of government term lending to small businesses and of commercial bank term lending have always been intertwined. The government and banks started to make term loans to businesses at about the same time, 1933–1934, because of changes brought on by the great depression. Since then there has never been a time when the two sectors did not share the term loan market. The development of this market has been dominated by the increasing sophistication of private sector services and their expansion to a wider range of business clients. One theme throughout this period has been the government's support for private sector development. The government substituted for the financial sector when it faltered, prodded it toward important innovations, and filled in permanently in areas the private system could not serve. Business credit programs have been one of the government's tools.

The reverse side of this theme, which is more immediately relevant for our purposes, concerns the effect of private development on government credit programs. The increasing abilities of the private sector have gradually diminished the need for the government itself to provide credit. The history of government business loan programs is therefore one of gradual, creative retreat. The current SBA loan guarantee program represents the end to date of that process. Among the most important questions facing SBA today is what justifies the government's continued presence in a market private banks have largely learned to serve. A review of the events in the development of the SBA program will show that growing bank abilities have tended to weaken the original clear need for government intervention.

COMMERCIAL BANKING AND THE RECONSTRUCTION
FINANCE CORPORATION, 1932 TO 1953

At the start of 1932 the commercial banking industry was struggling with losses on loans to borrowers who had become insolvent. They suffered withdrawal of depositor confidence—and money. As part of the general economic collapse the volume of business lending had been decreasing steadily. Between 1929 and 1932 the volume of loans made annually by commercial banks fell 44 percent, reversing the steady growth trend that had characterized the first part of the century.[1] To increase depositor confidence, banks lent a smaller proportion of their available funds. Even had they desired to lend more, businesses frequently offered poor prospects for repayment in the deflationary, low-demand economy. Recovery from the banking crisis was slow; for the rest of the decade loan volume stayed below its dismal 1932 level.[2]

The federal government responded to the financial collapse in several ways. The changes in the regulatory framework for financial institutions, which enabled a modern financial system to develop, are well known. Even before this, however, the government became an emergency source of business finance. The Reconstruction Finance Corporation (RFC) was created in 1932, during the Hoover administration, to provide emergency capital to commercial banks. In 1934 its powers were extended to include loans to nonfinancial businesses. This extension of RFC authority to businesses is appropriately considered the beginning of the present SBA 7(a) loan guarantee program; when the RFC was closed the SBA was created in 1953 to assume its basic business loan function.

The RFC made medium- and some long-term business loans, both directly and in participation with private banks. Loans to nonfinancial businesses were not the heart of RFC's initial operation, nor did they at first involve the large sums required for its program of aid to failing financial institutions. After the initial financial crisis cooled, however, business lending emerged as the central activity of the corporation, and remained so until SBA replaced it.

In fulfilling its mission RFC was to support and supplement commercial bank operations, but not to compete directly with them. The original purposes of the business loan authority were to serve local markets that had been left without their normal sources of credit by bank failures, and to help businesses whose capital had been used up during the years of decline.[3] The prohibition against competing with banks had been incorporated into RFC's mandate by a provision that it make loans only "to solvent business enterprises unable to obtain credit through normal channels."[4] RFC was left with the task of deciding when normal channels were not available.

In the initial period, when commercial banks were not lending actively, RFC could be confident that most loans it made would be a net addition to those of private lenders. As financial conditions gradually improved, banks began to loan more extensively. RFC's effort to avoid direct competition in the face of changes in private financial markets drove its policy throughout the next two decades. It required successive generations of purposes and procedures. RFC changed both the types of firms it lent to and the credit forms it used.

The best example of this kind of RFC interaction with banks is the development of medium- and long-term loans. Before the early 1930s most commercial bank business credit took the form of overdrafts or lines of credit, almost all of which matured in a year or less. The 90-day rolling overdraft has always been the industry's routine way of providing business loans. This followed from a philosophy that commercial banks were primarily suppliers of seasonal credit, and that businesses should be otherwise independently financed.[5] Even though banks often repeatedly renewed overdrafts, they did not make explicit commitments for longer than a year. Self amortizing term loans were rarely seen. Bank loans were simply not a way to finance major investments, start-ups or expansions.

In the early 1930s it was clear that businesses needed longer term credit in order to recover. This need prompted RFC to make loans of five to ten year maturities. Banks began exploring this innovation at the same time. They were motivated, like RFC, in part by increased demand by businesses for longer maturities. They became more willing to meet the demand because alternative term investments, particularly securities, had become less attractive. Skittishness in the stock and bond markets, and the new SEC requirements, had reduced yields on securities. There was some movement away from them by both issuing firms and financiers. They became more able to meet the demand through the development of new ways of stabilizing deposit levels, including federal deposit insurance and the ability to borrow from the Federal Reserve system. Finally, bank examiners began to give banks permission to move into this new market.[6]

Banks began term lending cautiously, starting with the most secure firms and only slightly increasing maturities. According to some observers, the business loans of RFC and a similar program of the Federal Reserve played a significant role in the development of the private term loan function, even though the programs were small relative to total bank lending.

The activities of the Federal Reserve banks and of the Reconstruction Finance Corporation in making term loans directly to business concerns helped set the stage for action by private financing agencies in these fields. It would be incorrect to say that the public agencies originated term lending, for there is evidence that a number of commercial banks made term loans prior to June 1934, at which time both Federal Reserve banks and the RFC were equipped with industrial loan powers. But indubitably the actions of these agencies educated many commercial banks in the techniques of making term loans.[7]

The nature of the influence was twofold. First, government loan programs demonstrated the effectiveness of various aspects of term lending, such as full amortization. Second, they encouraged banks to try out term lending for the first time in a protected way, by joint participation with the government. RFC at first lent money directly to businesses with no bank involvement. In the latter part of the 1930s it began to use joint participation, in which both a bank and RFC would advance a portion of a single loan (a practice already widespread among private banks for shorter term loans through the correspondent system). It had the authority to guarantee loans (called deferred participations), but did not use it frequently until after the war.

RFC's choice of credit type depended in large part on an assessment of how capable banks were of handling the risks RFC wished them to share. Even though it often worked with commercial banks, RFC differentiated its loans from those of private banks along several dimensions. It took on longer maturities. Maturities of commercial bank term loans rarely exceeded five years, while almost half of RFC loans had ten year terms, and some longer. Commercial banks tended to make loans to the larger firms, and this was especially true for term loans. RFC concentrated on smaller borrowers, though not the smallest. During the period from 1933 to 1940 RFC loans averaged $20,000 while commercial bank term loans averaged $644,000.[8] RFC also lent more to borrowers in southern and western states, areas with poorly developed financial sectors. On average it lent to borrowers with weaker balance sheets.

While banks selected the most promising clients, RFC's borrowers were selected with reference to national goals, first relief and then employment. During World War II RFC's size and authority were greatly expanded to support war production, and after the war the emphasis fell on developing new businesses. The general business lending program proved readily adaptable to such major shifts in national goals.

RFC also struggled with technical questions such as how much collateral a government agency should require, how it could determine whether credit would have been available without government assistance, and what form joint participation agreements with private lenders should take. There was a general movement throughout towards smaller loans, longer maturities, and more bank participation. SBA still deals with many of these technical issues today, though now with years of precedent behind it.

The major lesson to be drawn from RFC's experience is this: when it began, the failure in private financial capabilities that RFC business lending was called on to fill was undisputed, and the need of borrowers for the service RFC provided was as clear as the inability of commercial banks to provide it. When private banks became more able to make term loans, RFC was adaptable enough to turn its attention to national needs that were not being fully met, or to the outer limits of private abilities. In so doing, it made some contribution to extending those outer limits. It did not completely avoid direct competition with banks, however, as its postwar end shows.

CREATION OF THE SMALL BUSINESS ADMINISTRATION

By the late 1940s and early 1950s, the commercial banking industry was entering a period of vigorous expansion. Business loan demand was widely forecast to be high for an extended period. After almost two decades of experience with term loans, banks considered loans of three to five year maturities to be an essential part of their business services. From almost no term loans in 1933, the proportion of business loans with maturities over one year in 1940 had grown to approximately a third.[9] This proportion had increased during the war and remained high after it.

The banking industry began to argue that RFC was no longer needed. It was increasingly anxious to prevent RFC from becoming a direct competitor. At the same time management problems at RFC were receiving particular attention. Some RFC officials were accused of improprieties in loan decisions. The agency also faced controversy over its loan loss rates. RFC's business program had always generated a net loss, and this was a source of disagreement among policy makers. Some believed any subsidy to be unacceptable. Others objected to the level of loss as an indication of irresponsible management. Judgment about acceptable losses was made more confusing by the difficulty in documenting the actual loss suffered in a manner on which all parties could agree. About 10 percent of RFC business loans ended in default and foreclosure, according to one source.[10] The RFC was already liquidating its wartime operations, and it was clear that support for its more routine activities was weakening. Rather than continue only a portion of the activities, the Congress decided to liquidate the corporation.

Many of the participants in the decision to close the RFC were convinced that small businesses were the one type of borrower private lenders still served poorly. During the 1930s term loans had gone almost exclusively to large firms. Many banks had set minima on term loans at $50,000 or $100,000.[11] In 1942 some researchers doubted that it would ever be possible to finance small firms profitably because of economies of scale. Neil H. Jacoby and Raymond J. Saulnier of the National Bureau of Economic Research wrote that, "It seems unlikely that private agencies [banks and insurance companies] can profitably make term loans to the smallest corporations."[12]

In the years immediately following this judgment, banks developed installment loans for specific purchases, which were handled in essentially the same way for both businesses and consumers. These loans quickly became an important part of private bank portfolios. They also helped businesses finance equipment on favorable terms. By 1946 as much as 20 percent of the volume and 96 percent of the number of private term loans were smaller than $100,000, most of them under $10,000.[13] Banks were developing confidence that they could serve all small business needs.

The experts remained doubtful, however, particularly with regard to the financing of fixed plant and equipment assets not suitable for installment lending, loans for new firms, and loans requiring maturities over five years.[14] The Congress considered establishing a small business agency to continue the functions of RFC for businesses meeting certain size criteria. The legislation for a small business agency was supported by many small business associations, by the Republican administration, and by both Democrats and Republicans in Congress. Their testimony on behalf of the agency emphasized the lack of fair treatment small businesses faced in obtaining credit and the importance of small business for preserving free competition and the entrepreneurial character of the American economy.

The only open opponent of the bill to create the SBA was the American Bankers Association (ABA), the largest, most comprehensive banking lobby group. In testimony before the Senate Banking Committee, the chairman of the Association's small business credit committee stated,

Through the years, the American Bankers Association has consistently opposed the power of the Government and any of its agencies to make direct loans or to guarantee or insure business loans made by private financial institutions.[15]

Later in the same testimony he stated,

It seems almost incredible that we should be talking about Government credit needs of small business under the present healthy business conditions. The banks of this country are ready, willing and able to take care of the worthy credit needs of small business concerns.[16]

The ABA also raised a series of fairness and good government arguments. Among them were protests that firms receiving government credit would have an unfair advantage over their competitors, that funds would be used for political purposes and that government would be a poor and costly administrator.[17] Such protests continue to resurface in debate about the SBA.

Despite the opposition of the bankers, the Small Business Act passed easily in July 1953 (PL 83–163). It established the Small Business Administration, and gave it the power to make direct loans, loans in joint participation with banks, and loan guarantees. Though it was primarily to be a financing agency, it would also serve as the advocate for small business in government procurement and other matters. Opposition by the banks had been mitigated somewhat with insertion of the provision that SBA would be allowed to lend only to borrowers who did not meet commercial bank credit standards.[18]

Among the principles that were to guide the new agency, as cited by the administration in support of the legislation, were these: The agency should not compete with other lenders, but should support them. It should not provide financial assistance unless it is otherwise unavailable on reasonable terms. The loans extended should have "such value creditwise or [be] so secured as reasonably to assure repayment." In choosing recipients the agency should avoid businesses that "might offer unfair and dangerous competition to other businesses." Finally, the expenditure of federal funds should be kept to the minimum necessary for achieving the purposes of the agency.[19]

These principles define the need for and purpose of the SBA program in terms of the limits of private bank abilities, the same way RFC had been defined. SBA's legislation contained wording from RFC's legislation, such as that regarding reasonable safety and security, around which interpretive precedent had already grown. However, SBA's sphere of activity was smaller than RFC's, because the need for government action had narrowed. Explicitly, SBA was limited to smaller firms. In addition, the expansion of private bank activities had moved out the points at which prohibition against competition with banks became binding, so that the same legal wording resulted in a different actual practice. SBA's selection task was more difficult than RFC's, especially given its charge to minimize federal expenditures. The tension between a program justification based on serving a segment banks would not and a management concern to minimize costs and defaults is one of the central problems for SBA today.

DEVELOPMENTS IN THE BUSINESS LOAN PROGRAM

The statutory authority and administrative structure of SBA's business loan program now remain much as they were originally. The program has been remarkably stable for three decades. Within this legal framework it has made one major concession to the fact that bank abilities have expanded. It has moved away from direct and immediate participation loans toward guarantees. This has not entailed a change in borrowers targeted, but an increasing reliance on banks to carry out the administrative functions of the program. During SBA's first ten years guarantees were permitted, but used infrequently. In the early 1960s SBA increased guarantee volume such that by the end of the decade it extended more guarantees than direct loans. Guarantees continued to rise in importance throughout the seventies. At present the direct loan program is primarily used to fund loans to special types of borrowers. In 1986 its volume was only $160 million, compared to $2.8 billion for loan guarantees.

The most obvious reason for the change to guarantees is their budgetary

Table 1.1
SBA Guaranteed Loan Levels, 1954–1986 (in millions of dollars)

Year	New Loan Commitments	Outstanding Loans	Year	New Loan Commitments	Outstanding Loans
1954	128	3	1972	367	2,014
1956	132	31	1974	1,803	4,019
1958	167	48	1976	2,057	4,979
1960	159	56	1978	3,170	6,856
1962	172	62	1980	3,608	8,708
1964	70	81	1982	2,019	9,947
1966	147	159	1984	2,500	8,899
1968	314	441	1986	2,754	8,362
1970	446	808			

Source: Congressional Budget Office "Federal Credit Programs, A Statistical Compilation", in "Loan Guarantees: Current Concerns and Alternative for Control", Staff Working Papers, 1979, and Budget of the United States Government, Special Analysis F, "Federal Credit Programs", Fiscal Years 1982, 1984, 1986, and 1988.

advantage over direct loans. Guarantees use no government funds at the time they are issued, and only use them subsequently if default occurs. By contrast, direct loan funds come from the U.S. Treasury (if new lending exceeds receipts from repayments), leading to significant outlays in the year of disbursal. Charles Hertzberg, formerly second in command of the business loan program, and on SBA's staff for more than 20 years, observed,

It [the guarantee authority] existed for a long time, but it was very little used until sometime around 1967 when the demands of the Vietnam War changed the government's budgeting policy. . . . Outlay limitations were imposed and all of a sudden our guarantee program really started to gain popularity and usage.[20]

His words indicate that the focus on guarantees is almost a by-product of their budgetary treatment. However, it was not until the early 1970s that annual loan guarantee levels expanded rapidly (Table 1.1)

It is also clear that the move to guarantees makes banks more willing to support the program and fits the philosophy behind the program's creation. Guarantees have the advantages of using superior private funding and servicing abilities, and they help establish lasting borrower-bank relationships. If banks are able to raise funds and administer loans, use of those abilities agrees with the principle of avoiding competition between SBA and banks.

Another trend in SBA's business lending has been the development of programs aimed at special segments of the small business population, in accordance with the national popularity of certain causes. In the 1960s an economic opportunity program was created to lend to low income entrepreneurs. During the Carter administration a subprogram was created to lend to energy technology firms, and the Reagan administration has emphasized international trade. Unlike RFC's full-scale adaptation to national priorities, however, the SBA's basic business lending function has remained the same, with special purpose borrowers handled through small subprograms. In 1986 the list of special programs included, in addition to those just mentioned, handicapped assistance loans, local development company loans, pollution control loans, loans to veterans, and others. Most of these loans were made directly by SBA, rather than through guarantees. In 1986 the special programs accounted for only 8 percent of total guaranteed lending under SBA. It might be noted that loans to minorities have never been a separate program, though many of the economic opportunity loans went to minorities. SBA has tried to maintain the proportion of loans going to minorities at internally set target levels.

SBA's policies as to size of loans, maturities and borrower selection criteria have changed little since the first years of its existence. The average size of SBA loans increased from $65,000 in 1973 to $155,000 in 1986, but the upper bound set in legislation has not risen as much as inflation, having doubled from $250,000 to $500,000 since 1953. SBA has allowed some long-term loans, with maturities of up to 28 years, but most of its activity remains in the intermediate maturity category, between five and ten years.

During the same period the business loan function of commercial banks has continued to flourish. Term loans now account for approximately half of all commercial bank business loans. Sources of capital for term business finance, both through and outside of commercial banks have increased, especially with deregulation in financial markets. The commercial and industrial term loan function has settled into a regular pattern in terms of sizes, collateral requirements, and maturities (most between three and five years). Attitudes toward loan risk have changed little, however.

At present SBA loans can be distinguished from those of commercial banks primarily by being of longer maturity, on average, by going more often to newer firms and to minorities. They cannot be distinguished by type of industry or by size. In fact, the average size of SBA loans, which was $109,000 in 1982, is greater than the average size of commercial bank business loans, estimated in a 1981 survey of 224 banks to be $65,000.[21] Finally, even though the average maturities of bank term loans are shorter than SBA's, banks are nevertheless the source of most of the five to ten year loans that are extended.

The question of how SBA's program meshes with the array of private bank abilities continues to be important in assessing the success of the program. SBA serves a slightly different target group on slightly different terms than private banks. In the case of the RFC and the early SBA, policy makers believed that the financial system was inadequate for the task. This was clearly true at that time. Although flaws are now much less evident, the belief that private markets are flawed is still an important program justification. If financial markets are correct that SBA's target group is not creditworthy, SBA support for that group must be justified on other grounds. Chapter 5 evaluates these program justifications closely. It is important to note here that the belief that private markets are inadequate has been an important part of the origin and history of government small business lending.

POLITICAL SUPPORT FOR THE LOAN GUARANTEE PROGRAM

While the basic activities of the business loan program have remained very similar throughout the tenure of RFC and SBA, the program's political environment has changed in several fundamental ways. Among the major differences are increased support by the banking industry and the growth in importance of the nonlending functions of the SBA. These changes have a direct bearing on the political viability of the program. The rest of this chapter surveys the political forces that now surround the SBA program. It describes the interests of groups supporting the program and assesses the strength of their commitments to the program.

This discussion is based on the premise that two sets of goals motivate the activities and policies of any program: the explicit goals, which might be termed public interest goals, and the implicit goals pursued by the various parties involved with the program. Policy is debated, and will be evaluated in the later chapters of this book, in terms that appeal to some notion of the public interest. Actual decisions, however, often conform more closely to implicit motivations. When implicit interests conflict with public interests, the former usually prevail, and this makes the following discussion important for clarifying the opportunities and constraints awaiting any effort to improve the program.

Like beneficiaries of many government aid programs, borrowers from federal loan programs often form an organized and concerned group who attempt to improve their position through the program. An important point is that these groups shape the terms of debate so that their interests are presented as broad social interests. On the Export-Import Bank, for example, Jordan Jay Hillman writes that exporters

form a natural constituency that seeks, first, to establish the program and then to support increases in the quantity of goods or services provided on the most favorable terms possible. Its efforts will be to equate in the minds of Congress and public enterprise managers the growth of welfare benefits with the growth of resources allocated to the program.[22]

The beneficiaries succeed in promoting the identity of public and private interests because they often face no clear opposition. The costs and negative effects of most programs are diffused. No clear group is hurt noticeably, which frustrates development of a cohesive opposition. Low visibility of costs further lessens opposition. The costs of loan programs are particularly difficult to see because the programs generate their own revenues. In their financial statements, agencies may appear to be self-sustaining or nearly so, even when subsidies are present.

The SBA program is similar in that its costs are not easily noticed. However, it differs importantly from the standard model. Its beneficiaries, small business borrowers, are relatively weak as an interest group. Instead, service providers, the banks, who are not intended beneficiaries but are employed as vehicles for providing assistance, form a more effective constituency. Finally, members of the U.S Congress, particularly the Small Business Committees of both the House and the Senate, are the program's strongest effective constituency; they maintain the program with little organized, visible, external support.

This view of the program's support groups, which is elaborated in the next few pages, was developed on the basis of interviews with a high-ranking SBA official and the majority and minority staff directors of the two congressional small business committees and by review of the testimony presented to Congress on the program.

Borrowers as Constituents

When asked what the constituency of the 7(a) program is, both SBA and Congressional officials are likely to say, "small business." In actual practice, however, small business offers surprisingly little support for the program, for two main reasons.

First, small business is not a well-directed political force. There are too many small businesses, with interests and political views too diverse. A recent estimate states that there are 4.3 million small businesses in the country.[23] An estimated 86 percent of all firms in the United States can be classified as small. The millions of business people included here speak through a variety of organized lobby groups, the two most important of which are the National Association of Small Business (NASB) and the National Federation of Independent Businesses (NFIB). None of the associations can claim more than a small fraction of all firms as members. The associations even compete with each other to some extent, as they represent different shades of political opinion. Therefore, they are not very powerful at a national level. Small businesses are much more likely to be involved in a strong local, regional, or trade organization than one dominated by broad federal concerns.

Second, to the extent that small business is an effective political force, it channels its energies largely towards ends other than support for SBA's credit programs. Small business associations often testify before Congress in favor of the loan guarantee program, but, as Reagan administration officials have pointed out, the group as a whole is more concerned with general economic policy. An SBA administrator representing that administration's views stated,

Now in the Small Business Administration's case, we asked ourselves what are our constituents—the 12 to 16 million small businesses in the country—really interested in? We think clearly the answer is that they are interested in (1) curbing inflation, (2) access to credit at reasonable rates, (3) reduction in taxes, and (4) deregulation.[24]

Macroeconomic and tax issues affect nearly all association members. The SBA program helps only with access to credit, and only for a tiny proportion of all firms. In 1984, for example, it guaranteed approximately 17,000 loans, thus assisting 0.4 percent of all small firms. Over the course of five years it aids 2.2 percent at that rate. As a supplier of term loans it is relatively more important, but still affects a low proportion of all borrowing firms. At the end of 1983 it had guaranteed $9.5 billion in outstanding business loans, compared to $392 billion (in 1982) for commercial banks. If, as a recent survey found, 56 percent of commercial bank loans are to small business and half are term loans, commercial banks had an estimated $110 billion in term loans outstanding that year, more than ten times as many as SBA (though SBA terms are longer).

Occasionally the associations are more negative than positive. In 1979 a witness for NFIB testifying on the mission of SBA stated,

It is imperative the SBA realize it is not the center of the small business universe, for the major problems affecting its constituency are outside the scope of most of SBA's programs and activity.[25]

He then went on to recommend that the loan program be deemphasized. At the same hearing, a representative of NASB stated that SBA programs are not very relevant to the real mission of SBA to preserve and expand competition. The unfair advantage argument raised at the creation of SBA still surfaces today. Thriving small businesses do not wish to invite stronger competition by giving weaker firms government-backed loans. Some organizations also have difficulty supporting SBA because of a basic ideological orientation against government programs. The NFIB regularly polls its members on a variety of issues, including knowledge and use of the SBA and its programs. Its usual finding is that the loan guarantee program has low visibility among its members. In 1986 the NFIB polled its membership and received responses stating that the great majority of its members did not support the credit functions of SBA, but wished to keep SBA only as an advocate for small business within the government.

If all small businesses are not the program's real constituency, surely the actual recipients might be expected to protect it. But several factors prevent the businesses who receive SBA loans from joining together effectively. First, they are indistinguishable from nonrecipient firms in terms of size, industry, and location. Aside from the SBA they have no other unique common interest. Second, they are not what a member of a congressional Small Business Committee staff called a "continuous constituency." Most borrowers do not develop ongoing relationships with SBA. Their interest in the program ceases when their loans are disbursed. Therefore, individual recipients are little motivated to form special lobbying groups. Neither are future borrowers in a position to organize. They may not recognize themselves as such. As a result, there are no beneficiary groups proclaiming a large unmet demand for SBA loans.

The public support of SBA's 7(a) program by small businesses usually takes the form of anecdote. Individual business owners are often the only representatives of borrowers to speak on behalf of the program before Congress. They usually relate their own firm's experience with SBA. These witnesses frequently come from the states or districts of the members of Congress responsible for the hearings. Although they may belong to a local small business association, they do not claim to speak for the association.

This lack of beneficiary interest contrasts sharply with two other SBA programs, its guarantees of bonds issued to finance pollution control devices, and its small business investment company program. Both of these programs, though smaller than the 7(a) program, provide a subsidy to a readily identified group of firms. A large percentage of firms in the identified group actually receive SBA assistance. The first program provides an interest rate subsidy to firms that invest in pollution control equipment, and the other provides equity for investment companies (small business venture capital firms). The ease of identification of beneficiaries, the level of subsidy, and the ongoing dependence on SBA that accompany these programs have induced beneficiaries to form associations, the Small Business Coalition for Pollution Control, and the National Association of Small Business Investment Companies. The principal aims of these associations are to promote the continuation of their programs.

Racial and ethnic minority business owners are one beneficiary category that provide relatively strong support for the loan guarantee program, though it is largely a spillover from general support for SBA. Several SBA programs are directed primarily at minorities, including the Minority Enterprise Small Business Investment Companies (MESBIC) and the 8 (a) minority contracts program that provides assistance in obtaining federal procurement contracts. These have become two of SBA's most important programs. Moreover, the agency takes care that the minority share in benefits is substantial in all its programs. Minority support for the agency as a whole tends to benefit the loan guarantee program.

The general lack of beneficiary support groups affects policy making about the program. In the absence of a coordinated response from direct beneficiaries, attention turns away from the effect it has on borrowers toward other voices of concern, such as those of banks.

Banks as Constituents

Even though banks are ostensibly only vehicles for federal assistance, their influence on the program is stronger than the influence of beneficiaries. It is not unusual for service providers under government contracts to act as an interest group, attempting to influence a program's direction. In SBA's case, this has happened to such a degree that banks are almost seen as beneficiaries. One congressional staff member stated that banks were as much beneficiaries as small businesses, and two staff members offered continued demand for the program from banks as a main criterion for program success.

Numbers and level of involvement make banks a much more effective support group for the program than borrowers. While only a small percent of all small businesses participate in the SBA program, over two-thirds of all commercial banks participate. Even if only active banks (with more than 10 loans) are counted, SBA affects 20 percent, and among the 20 percent are almost all of the largest, most influential banks. Moreover, while most businesses borrow only once from SBA, active banks develop ongoing relationships and expertise.

Banks offer public support for the continuation and expansion of the program. The American Bankers Association has long since dropped its opposition to the business loan program, co-opted in effect by the transition to guarantees. SBA has solved the political problems caused by competing with banks by giving them a share in the program. The ABA describes the program in publications as an accepted and perhaps necessary part of the range of small business financing methods, though it still opposes direct loans.

However, while the support from banks for this program is stronger than that from small business groups, there are similar reservations, largely because bank groups consider other legislative and public policy concerns far more important. In particular, these include monetary policy and bank regulation. Hertzberg summarized the attitude of banks to the program in the following way:

I think they have been supportive, maybe in a self interested way. Those that have been using the programs are very supportive. American Bankers has been very cooperative. The Independent Bankers Association has been cooperative and supportive. They are kind of reserved in what they say to Congress. They save it for such things as withholding of taxes in savings accounts. They want to save their chips.[26]

The repeated attempts by the Reagan administration to reduce or abolish the loan guarantee program helped spark the creation of a bank association made up solely of active SBA lenders, the National Association of Government Guaranteed Lenders (NAGGL). This group now takes its place on the witness stand whenever the loan guarantee program is debated, and follows every detail of program administration.

Banks work quietly with SBA staff on specific program issues. It is through this detailed work that banks leave a strong imprint on the structure and evolution of the program. The individuals in charge of the largest SBA portfolios are quite familiar to the managers of the SBA program in Washington, with whom they confer about their specific problems as well as about issues that affect the whole program. The ABA's small business credit committee meets regularly with SBA officials to discuss how to improve the program. Bankers dominated the Small Business Committee on Capital Access, an advisory group appointed by SBA in 1981 whose agenda for improving the program has been the basis for much of SBA's subsequent action.

The aims of banks in supporting the program are, of course, not the same as those of borrowers, and the program reflects this. Banks seek changes that will make the program generate a higher return on assisted loans, help attract customers, and provide income. Some banks view it as a marketing and expansion tool, a way to try out new customers at low risk. The extent to which these aims coincide with SBA's interests will be an important concern of later chapters.

One other service provider group deserves mention. Because of SBA's secondary market, brokers who find investors for the loans banks wish to sell have testified in favor of the program frequently in recent years. While they are a highly motivated and compact group, most of their interest in the program centers on improving the secondary market.

Congressional Small Business Committees

Although there is some external support for the 7(a) program, it does not appear to be unyielding support. In light of this it is surprising that the program has continued for so long. It is my hypothesis that one of the main reasons it continues to survive is that it meets certain needs of the Congressmen and Senators on the House and Senate Small Business Committees who oversee the programs. These needs are served without the help of an organized external constituency. In effect, the small business committees are the most important constituent group.

This hypothesis is based on the responses by each of the SBA and congressional staff members interviewed to the question, "What groups offer the strongest support for the program?" In each case, the interviewees immediately named the committees. Major Clark, former staff director for the House Small Business Committee, stated that the committee itself had been "the main voice of support" for the program.[27] The Senate committee's staff director concurred, and went further, saying that the committees felt no need for external support because they were firm in their commitment. When asked what groups reacted when reductions in the program were suggested, SBA's Hertzberg replied, "Basically, the Congress."[28] All of the interviewees placed the committees first, the banks second, and small business third in level of commitment to the program. A frequently cited example is that when the Reagan administration suggested deep cuts in the program in 1981 and 1982 the committees went their own ways with no attempt to mobilize interest groups. In 1982, for example, Congress heard no testimony on the program from representatives of business organizations.

It is easier to observe that members of Congress maintain the program with little organized external pressure than it is to explain why they do. A brief investigation of the nature of the two small business committees and of the program itself provides the basis for conjecture as to the benefits the program provides them.

The small business committees have a small legislative jurisdiction relative to most other House and Senate committees, and in several senses the loan guarantee program has been the core of that jurisdiction. As such it is carefully guarded. The committees began primarily as advocates for small business and originally had no legislative powers. They were created in the 1940s as select committees to study the special problems of small business. Today the committees spend most of their time holding hearings on issues falling into one of three categories: the role of small business in the economy, the effect on small business of major economic developments, and the impact on small business of federal government programs and regulations. Few of these involve programmatic legislation.

In 1974 (House) and 1976 (Senate) the committees were given jurisdiction over the SBA and Small Business Act. Any legislation they propose must be written as an amendment to that act, and if it has an administrative component, this is assigned to SBA. The Senate committee had to fend off a 1976 recommendation by the Stevenson Committee on reorganization of the Senate to abolish it. It obtained jurisdiction over SBA as the outcome of the ensuing struggle, which was strongly supported by organized small business. The members may, therefore, regard the committee's jurisdiction over SBA as its claim to permanence. As long as this is maintained, the committee has a base from which to pursue the kind of work dealing with national economic and industrial issues that one committee staff member described as "more glamorous." The committees protect the SBA and its programs because, although small, it is their only slice of the federal budget.

If it is granted that the committees have a strong interest in maintaining the SBA, it follows that the loan guarantee program is highly likely to receive support. Within the SBA, the loan guarantee program is the most important activity, in terms of dollars of assistance given and numbers of businesses aided. In addition to its dollar volume, it provides the organizational structure for the agency. When SBA began, the loan program was its major function. Its extensive branch network was primarily oriented toward supplying finance. Other programs have since grown in importance, including disaster and procurement assistance, but business finance remains the heart of branch operations. As one congressional staff member reported, cutting out or substantially reducing the loan guarantee program would be tantamount to a major restructuring of the agency itself.

The relative importance of business loans within SBA has been on an extended, gradual decline; procurement, investment, and advocacy activities have gained importance. The biggest threat to the business loan program may be that the other SBA programs grow to the point that the business loan program is no longer seen as the center of agency activities.

A separate explanation for committee loyalty to the loan guarantee program despite weak organizational support lies in the effect of the program at the state and local level, that is, within home states and Congressional districts. The SBA program operates in each district. Within each district it affects people who are relatively prominent in comparison with the average voter: bankers and local entrepreneurs. (Former President Carter was once an SBA loan recipient.) SBA borrowers are much more likely to be involved in a business organization that plays a significant role in local or regional political events than in national ones. Several Congressional staff members noted that the regional small business organizations were often stronger than the national ones, and more supportive of SBA.

Both members of the two committees and members of Congress in general can benefit from the local impact of the SBA program. Bankers and local entrepreneurs are likely to be influential in voter opinion, and even important campaign contributors. Congressmen maintain staff members who intervene directly on behalf of constituents to smooth bureaucratic delays or otherwise assist them to obtain benefits from the federal government. The SBA program lends itself well to such intervention. A recommendation from a Congressman can help a business owner obtain an SBA loan, or can appear to help. A Congressman can make good use of a few stories of successful businesses who received SBA loans.

From time to time there have been charges that Congressional or other political influence in selection of SBA loan recipients in some districts has been heavy to the point of impropriety. No evidence is presented here either to support or deny such claims, but the fact that they are made shows that some people believe the program to be tied to local political benefits.

Potential local constituency benefits help explain the broad Congressional support for the program, which has always been bipartisan. The members of the small business committees would receive the same benefits as other Congressmen, though to a greater degree. A major motivation for joining the committee is likely to be a desire to show responsiveness to the local business community.

Many other federal programs can equal or surpass SBA's in demonstrating district responsiveness by representatives. Examples include defense contracts and water projects, among others. Thus, even on this count, the program's backing would not be of the strongest. In view of this, a final reason for the program's continuation is the lack of any significant opposition. The array of supporting forces inside and outside the Congress is not overwhelmingly strong, but it is strong enough to keep the program going by inertia. No particularly strong force has appeared that would throw it off its course. Like many other federal programs, no one will clearly benefit from reducing or ending the program though many will clearly be hurt.

The program has two additional features that tend to dampen opposition. First, promoting small business is an almost universally applauded activity. Both Republicans and Democrats praise small business as a source of many of the best attributes of the American economy and society. Some on the right object to the subsidy or to government involvement, but this is mitigated because the program uses guarantees and commercial banks, and is therefore less interventionist than most. The second opposition dampening feature is that there are few budget savings to come from reducing or ending the guarantee program. Government funds are only used to cover default losses, a fraction of the total program loan volume.

A brief statement of the Congressional objectives for this program would be to reach the largest possible number of potentially influential citizens at a low budget cost. As long as it continues to do this, and is not superseded by other SBA activities, the program is likely to survive.

The SBA Bureaucracy and the Administration

Two other governmental groups are concerned with the fate of the guarantee program, the SBA bureaucracy and the central portions of the executive branch—the administration. The SBA bureaucracy's general position of support for program continuation has been steady, except when it has been pressured to act otherwise by the central administration. As noted, the program is central to SBA's organizational structure. The central administration, however, may or may not be supportive. The Carter administration generally looked on the program favorably. The only real opposition to the program in recent times has come from the budgetary side of the Reagan administration. According to one congressional staff member, the "credit control ideologues" in the Treasury and Office of Management and Budget were responsible for recommendations for substantial cutbacks in each budget submitted by the Reagan administration. This opposition is founded on antigovernment intervention grounds. While they have not succeeded in abolishing the program, as was proposed in 1986, their strong opposition helped congeal forces for a set of program reforms that tighten program rules. In most other years, however, Congress ignored the recommended cutbacks.

EFFECTS OF INTEREST GROUP FORCES ON POLICIES

The nature and strength of interest group support for the SBA program have predictable effects on the way the program is designed and run. The relative weakness of business groups is reflected in a lack of attention at a policy level to who borrowers are, how the loans affect them, and how their businesses fare subsequently. By contrast, a great deal of effort is spent to improve the program's interface with participating banks. The interests of Congressmen in using the program in home districts is reflected in broadly inclusive eligibility rules. Finally, the sum of support from all sources for this program is not massive or vehement, and the program depends in large part on the lack of effective opposition. This balance of support is reflected in program levels which have remained static throughout the 1980s. A brief review of trends in program policies illustrates these points.

During the past decade the program has grown more slowly than the budget as a whole. It has declined slightly during the 1980s, not again reaching its high of $3.6 billion in new commitments, achieved in 1980. The consensus between Democrats and Republicans in Congress that the program should continue has protected it from administration attempts to cut it or to phase it out. In 1981, a year of strong Reagan administration assault on the budget, the Congress sacrificed the direct loan program, which reaches far fewer borrowers, shows higher current outlays, and has no bank support, in order to preserve the loan guarantee program.

In the absence of major controversies over the program's future, one focus of committee energies during this time was the details of program regulations and administrative questions, such as loan servicing procedures and size limitations. Ideological differences can surface quickly on some of these questions, even if the basic support for the program is bipartisan. Two of the most important of these have been the minimum guarantee percentage and the maximum allowable interest rate. These are fertile issues for partisan clashes. One side wishes to give private lenders full discretion, trusting the market, while the other wishes to protect borrowers from unscrupulous lenders. Such disputes can sometimes fill large amounts of committee time.

Major efforts to improve the program have concerned ways to make it more attractive to the better organized of its external support groups, the banks. Congressional staff report greater reliance on the private sector as the major programmatic thrust in the 1980s. The two largest program innovations in the past decade have been the development of the secondary market and the certified lender program, both designed to make the guaranteed loans more attractive to banks. Both these programs were supported by the SBA during the SBA's Reagan-appointed leadership. Most legislative and administrative innovations affecting the program in the 1980s have dealt with expansion and improvement of these programs. These reforms continue the gradual retreat of government involvement in favor of private lenders that began under RFC.

The agenda for these improvements was developed by the group of small businessmen, bankers, and securities dealers appointed in 1981 to the Small Business Committee on Capital Access. For the secondary market the Capital Access Committee's recommendations included pooling loans for sale and covering them with a guarantee of timely repayment, so that they would trade more like Government National Mortgage Association securities than like bank loans. Before this guarantee, loans were traded individually through brokers, and are less marketable than securities: this reduced their yield to the originating banks who sold them. For the certified lender program an earlier recommendation to turn over more decision-making authority to banks resulted in the creation of the preferred lender program. The preferred lender program, a refinement of the certified lender program, gives banks with proved performance the authority to make SBA guaranteed loans without prior individual loan approval from SBA.

It may seem ironic that in a program whose annual level is legislatively constrained, and for whose expansion there is no strong voice, so much effort should be put into increasing its attractiveness to banks. Ostensible reasons are that decision makers consider placing greater responsibility in the hands of private lenders as an end in itself, and hope that borrowers will receive benefits in the form of lower interest rates. Another motivation may stand behind these reforms, however. As Clark pointed out, if more banks find the program attractive, the strength of their support will increase, and it will be easier for program supporters to demonstrate that demand for the program warrants its expansion. The reforms build a better external constituency.

After five years in which Congress easily rebuffed cutback proposals from the administration, and the SBA allowed the special programs to develop as described, the Reagan administration made a final, concerted attempt to do away with both the loan guarantee program and SBA. This was probably the strongest challenge SBA faced since its inception. The charge, led by Budget Director Stockman, was accompanied by a well-publicized Heritage Foundation critique of SBA's loan guarantee program and followed by the appointment as Administrator of Mr. Charles Heatherly, who viewed his task as the dismantling of SBA. The proposal was to terminate all SBA credit programs, and transfer SBA's remaining functions to the Department of Commerce. In response to the proposals, the small business associations staunchly defended the SBA. But, as described above, they were far more interested in preserving the independent advocacy function of SBA than in saving the loan programs. This shows both the weak support of organized business for the guarantee program and the waning centrality of the program among all of SBA's activities. The NFIB initially agreed to support the elimination of the loan guarantee program in return for a retraction by the administration of the proposal to move advocacy into the Commerce Department. In the end, banks (including the ABA and NAGGL) as well as Congress (supported by the stories of more than 50 successful SBA loan recipients) preserved the loan guarantee program and most other functions of SBA. However, this time, the combination of attack from the administration and public criticism originating from the Heritage Foundation report were sufficient to convince Congress that something had to be done. The Congress accordingly raised the guarantee fee from 1 to 2 percent, as a cost-saving measure, and reduced the guarantee percentage for certain types of loans, both being improvements in the program. It also authorized SBA for three years, protecting it from further attack by the Reagan administration.

Areas of Little Policy Focus

Two crucial areas were conspicuously lacking in the policy developments of the 1980s: borrowers and defaults. The two goals of program decision makers, to increase bank participation and to reach a large number of borrowers at low cost, led them to overlook the actual outcome of the program, in terms of the number of successful loans and the impact of loans on borrowers. The number of loans has been stressed as a target more than has the success rate of loans. Nor have there been any recent attempts to target specific types of borrowers or to restrict the way firms use SBA loans. Even the existing special purpose programs have been waning in importance. In addition to appealing to Congressmen, this lack of restriction may be desired by banks, who wish to retain discretion. As a result, little is known about the impact of SBA guaranteed loans on borrowers.

In keeping with the lack of attention given to final outcomes, the level of default in the program has not become a significant issue. As one staff member put it, defaults are usually thought of as an administrative issue. A member of the House Small Business Committee staff asserted that as the level of defaults was low, in the opinion of most members of Congress and their staff, there had never been any need to discuss what an appropriate level of defaults might be. An SBA official reported that if Congress did not take up the issue of the appropriate default level it would not be the place of the administration to do so. The guarantee program receives little scrutiny on this issue because its default rate is eclipsed by extremely high default rates (above 40 percent) for some of the direct loan and economic opportunity loan programs. Nonetheless, a concern with budget outlays generated by defaulting guarantees, $523 million in 1986, led the Reagan administration to adopt a policy of increasing loan "quality" in which SBA field offices were directed to be more selective in approving loan applications.

With these comments on the effect of various groups on the policies of the SBA program, we leave the historical and political background, and begin analysis of the program's financial performance. For the subsequent evaluation, one of the most important ideas to come from the historical and political review is the central role of banks in determining the nature of the program. It is by reference to bank failings that the program has been justified, and it is banks who set much of the agenda for specific reforms SBA has pursued. An essential part of evaluating the SBA program is understanding how it affects the normal operating procedures of banks, and what rate of return it brings them. Finally, the political forces surrounding the program set practical limits to potential program reform. Just as they explain why the program has certain seemingly nonuseful features, such as a high default rate, these forces can help predict the likely reaction to proposed changes.

NOTES

1. Paul Studenski and Herman E. Krooss, *Financial History of the United States*, 2nd ed. (New York: McGraw-Hill, 1963), p. 370.

2. Ibid., p. 400.

3. Neil H. Jacoby and Raymond J. Saulnier, *Business Finance and Banking* (New York: National Bureau of Economic Research, 1947), p. 122.

4. Raymond J. Saulnier, Harold G. Halcrow and Neil H. Jacoby, *Federal Lending and Loan Insurance*, National Bureau of Economic Research (Princeton: Princeton University Press, 1958), p. 422.

5. Jacoby and Saulnier, *Business Finance*, p. 12.

6. Ibid., p. 2.

7. Ibid., p. 24.

8. Ibid., p. 34.

9. Ibid., p. 1.

10. Jesse H. Jones with Edward Angly, *Fifty Billion Dollars: My Thirteen Years with the RFC* (New York: Macmillan, 1951).

11. Jacoby and Saulnier, *Business Finance*, p. 109.

12. Ibid., p. 35.

13. Saulnier, Halcrow, and Jacoby, *Federal Lending*, p. 247.

14. Testimonies of Federal Reserve, Smaller Business of America, Inc., National

Federation of Independent Business, Council of Independent Business, and others, U.S. Congress, Senate Committee on Banking and Currency, *Government Lending Agencies*, Hearings, 83rd Cong., 1st sess., May 1953.

15. Ibid., pp. 290–91.

16. Ibid., p. 295.

17. Ibid., p. 292.

18. Statement of E. Reese, vice-president, American Bankers Association, U.S. Congress, House Committee on Banking and Currency, *Creation of Small Business Administration*, Hearings, 83rd Cong., 1st sess., May 1953, pp. 63–67.

19. Testimonies of K. R. Cravens (RFC Administrator) and Burgess W. Randolph (Deputy Secretary of the Treasury) in *Government Lending Agencies*, pp. 60 and 86.

20. Interview with Charles Hertzberg, October 1983.

21. Cynthia Glassman and Peter L. Struck, "Survey of Commercial Bank Lending to Small Business" (Washington, D.C.: Interagency Task Force on Small Business Finance, January 1982), p. 40.

22. Jordan Jay Hillman, *The Export-Import Bank at Work: Promoting Financing in the Public Sector* (Westport, Conn.: Quorum Books, 1982), p. xiv.

23. Small Business Administration, *The State of Small Business: A Report of the President* (Washington, D.C.: GPO, March 1983), p. 201.

24. Roger H. Jones, acting SBA administrator, U.S. Congress, House Committee on Small Business, *SBA Legislation and Programs*, Hearings, 97th Cong., 1st sess., March 1981, p. 5.

25. Senate Committee on Small Business, *Examination of the Mission of SBA*, Hearings, 95th Cong., 1st sess., October 1977, pp. 216–17.

26. Interview with Charles Hertzberg, October 1983.

27. Interview with Major Clark, March 1984.

28. Interview with Charles Hertzberg, October 1983.

2 The Life Cycle of SBA Loans

The SBA loan guarantee program was set up on the premises that banks were too risk averse, that there were plenty of good small businesses, and that the country should bet on some of these, even if banks would not. One would expect that a program established under such reasoning would tolerate a somewhat higher rate of failure among its borrowers than private banks in normal commerce. However, as it happens, the failure rate is not just somewhat higher, but of an entirely different order of magnitude. In fact, SBA borrowers default about ten times as often as comparable private bank customers; nearly one in four loans goes sour.

The frequency of failure has a great deal to do with whether the SBA program is good public policy. The number of defaults, their costs, the circumstances in which they occur, and the actions taken to remedy them are all basic indicators of whether the program is working well. For the most part, however, the importance of the default rate has not been emphasized in public discourse. SBA itself has made little effort to discover and discuss what the rate of failure actually is. The one in four figure just quoted is the finding not of SBA but of an analysis performed by the author, to be discussed in this chapter. More importantly, neither SBA nor policy makers have seriously questioned whether actual performance is acceptable. The actual default performance of SBA loans has direct implications—costs—for banks, borrowers and the SBA. Until these are understood and weighed against program benefits, there is too little basis to judge whether the SBA program is successful and ought to continue.

The main concern of this chapter is how SBA-guaranteed loans behave with respect to repayment and default. Subsequent chapters will use the picture of SBA loan behavior developed in this chapter as a foundation

Table 2.1
Status of Guaranteed Loans Outstanding (end of fiscal year 1984, in millions of dollars)

Loan Status	----Bank Loans---- $	%	--Purchased Loans- $	%	------Total------ $	%
Current	6383	89.1	221	12.7	6604	74.2
Deferred	50	0.7	22	1.3	72	0.8
Past due (1-60 days)	297	4.1	33	1.9	330	3.7
Delinquent (60 or more days) a/	334	4.7	159	9.2	493	5.5
Liquidation a/	101	1.4	1300	74.9	1401	15.7
	----	----	----	----	----	----
Total	7165		1735		8900	100.0
Percent of total	80.5	100.0	19.5	100.0	100.0	

Source: SBA Management Information Survey, October 1984, p. 1b.

a/ Eligible for purchase.

for assessing the financial effect of the program on banks, borrowers, and SBA, and for discussing possibilities for program improvement.

SBA'S LOAN PERFORMANCE DATA

SBA provides information on default to the public in very abbreviated form in the annual U.S. Budget and in its own annual report. These documents show how much money SBA spends each year to buy failing loans. This can be compared to the total amount of loans outstanding to give a rough picture of program performance. In 1986, for example, SBA spent $523 million to purchase loans. As total guaranteed loans outstanding that year were $8.4 billion, this means that 6.3 percent of the loans defaulted in that year. SBA also reports the total of purchased loans it holds, in its Management Information Survey, which is not regularly released to the public (Table 2.1). That survey has more revealing information than the Budget, but is still a snapshot approach. As of the end of 1984 purchased loans (loans in default) were 19.5 percent of the total number of loans outstanding.

While changes in these numbers can signal trends from year to year, they are not the indicators most useful in assessing SBA policy, the long-run rates of loan failure. The published figures are clouded with extraneous information. First, they are given in terms of dollar volume, rather than number of loans purchased. Purchases are usually smaller than the original loan amount, because portions of the loans have already been repaid. This means that the dollar percentage is less than the percentage expressed in numbers of loans. From a policy standpoint, it is important to know both how much defaults cost and how many businesses are failing. Second, at any given time, the ratio of bad loans to the total loan portfolio is affected by the age mix of the loans in it and by current economic conditions. Loans only begin to default in large numbers during the second and third years of their lives. Therefore, as long as the program is growing, a ratio of current defaults to current outstandings will always appear artificially low, and casual observers will be unaware of the real magnitude of the default problem. This has been the case throughout much of SBA's history. Third, business cycle peaks and troughs change current default performance significantly from the long-run average.

In order to make the extensive data SBA collects more useful for evaluation of policy concerns, SBA's loan performance data was analyzed extensively for this study. The findings on the default rate discussed in this chapter result from analysis of the performance of over 120,000 SBA loans disbursed in the years 1973 through 1983. This is more than three quarters of all loans SBA guaranteed during that time, and so the analysis represents a very comprehensive look at the program. To my knowledge, this is one of a very few times the aggregate performance of SBA loans has been examined in detail, particularly by an analyst outside of SBA. The data were provided by SBA from its own loan tracking system. SBA maintains quite complete computerized files on the status of each of its guaranteed loans. It records status information on each loan from date of initial disbursement through final disposition, be that normal repayment or charge off. Unfortunately, however, SBA has done little to exploit the potential such data holds for explaining the program's dynamics. The only analysis of the loan history data known to the author was carried out in 1980 and 1981 by SBA's chief actuary, J. Ramon Estefania, but SBA did not release this to the public.

The analysis performed for this study isolated three distinct aspects of SBA loan behavior, and examined each in turn. The first stage of analysis incorporated an actuary's view of the program and examined the loans according to their ages, or time elapsed since they were disbursed. Each group of loans made in a single month was followed from the start of their lives to maturity, with other things, particularly economic conditions, held constant. The technique used was the construction of a hazard model, which plots the transition of a population from one state to another over time. The first stage of the analysis yielded the long-run expected rate of failure. In the second stage of the analysis, loan age was held constant, and the links between likelihood of default and business cycle conditions were examined, using multiple regression analysis. Finally, a third stage in the analysis looked more closely at a subsample of 8,250 loans that were purchased. Parameters were investigated such as the time between first delinquency and the ultimate charge off of the loan by SBA and the ratio of original principal to principal eventually charged off. Again, a hazard model was used. Readers interested in the analytic techniques used or in details of the findings summarized here should refer to the appendix, where these are described at greater length.

The end result of the analysis is a succinct and highly detailed model of the life cycle of SBA loans that can be used to understand a great deal about the SBA program and about longer term commercial lending generally. The model can be used to examine how borrowers and lenders respond to the incentives built into the program, and it can be helpful in predicting the effect on the program of changes in policy, management, or economic conditions. For commercial lending generally, the model can act as a magnifying lens for inspection of the nature of credit risk, by virtue of the extensive data on which the analysis is based. It is rare that such a numerous and well-documented portfolio of loans, made over a significant stretch of time, by banks all over the country, is available for analysis. Even if such a data set were available for private bank loans, it would be difficult to study defaults because they occur so infrequently among private borrowers. The defaults among SBA loans serve as an enlargement of a phenomenon normally difficult to see. While many more SBA loans than private loans default, the timing and pattern of default is likely to be similar. SBA loans can provide insight into defaulting loans in general.

We turn next to the results of this analysis. The next section discusses how often defaults occur, and the section following that discusses the disposition of loans that default.

THE TIMING AND FREQUENCY OF DEFAULT

Loan Purchase

The best indicator of default for SBA loans, and the one examined here, is loan purchase, when SBA buys a failing loan from a bank. In any lending operation, default may be defined as the time at which it becomes clear that the borrower will not fulfill his repayment obligations. From the borrower's point of view, default is not a single event, but a process of decline punctuated by changes in the way the lender handles the loan. It is somewhat arbitrary to name the exact point at which a loan should be considered in default; the timing and use of remedial action often require subjective judgment. Private banks usually define default not by a specific point, but by placing loans in successively deteriorating categories, according to variables such as the time passed since the borrower stopped regular repayment. Fortunately for the sake of analysis, default can be defined more distinctly for SBA loans, as the exercise of the guarantee. When the bank calls the guarantee, SBA purchases the loan. This transfer of ownership places a clear before and after marker on an otherwise somewhat subjective definition. Moreover, because they involve SBA expenditures, SBA records purchases carefully, generating readily usable information. For this reason, this analysis equates default among SBA loans with purchases, and uses the terms interchangeably.

Purchase occurs at the option of the bank. Whenever a borrower is over 60 days in arrears, that is, has missed two monthly payments, the lender can call the guarantee agreement into effect. On demand, SBA immediately purchases the guaranteed portion of the loan's currently outstanding principal. For a 90 percent guaranteed loan, SBA writes a check for 90 percent of the current balance (not the original loan amount), plus 90 percent of the unpaid interest that has accrued during the period of delinquency. Thereafter, SBA owns the loans and has responsibility for collection, though it must share any subsequent recovery with the bank in the original guarantee proportion. After purchase, some repayments may be received, but most loans are eventually charged off.

As a comparison to private commercial terminology, purchase comes close to what banks call gross charge off. According to industry analysts Robert Morris Associates, banks eventually recover about 26 percent of principal classified as gross charge offs.[1] For SBA loans, recoveries after purchase have totaled about 30 percent.

Purchase is also important because the decision of whether and when the guarantee claim should be exercised is one of the chief delegations of authority SBA gives to banks. The circumstances in which purchases occur are therefore important indicators of how well banks fulfill their managerial responsibilities.

In this discussion we will be concerned primarily with the numbers of loans that are purchased and their final disposition, and only secondarily with the amount of principal lost. The number of defaults is a far more important indicator of success to SBA than it would be to a private bank, because the objectives of each differ. A bank's profit orientation would lead it to be concerned primarily with the amount of its loss, and thus with its final charge off rate. Because SBA's objectives are so strongly social, SBA cares about the fate of its borrowers. In general, a purchased loan means a failed borrower. Except in what are believed to be fairly infrequent cases of deliberate nonpayment, a default represents a business that has been unable to meet its minimal obligations. Most defaults result in the loss by the owner of his or her business and perhaps personal assets, a high individual cost. For SBA, a default represents an expenditure that has not contributed to the objectives of the program of promoting business start up and expansion, but rather a cost that must be compensated for by the benefits other, successful loans generate. For judging the relative cost and benefit of the SBA program, a low long-run proportion of defaulters would be preferred to a higher one even if both produced the same final dollar charge offs, because it would mean more successful firms.

Long-Run Rate of Default

If one views the SBA program in the aggregate in any given year, the long-run default or purchase rate cannot be readily determined. In order to unclutter the picture and calculate that figure, it is helpful to look at what happens to a group of similar maturity loans, all made at the same time, as they progress through their life cycle. All the loans will be outstanding at first, but as time passes, loans will be retired, either through full repayment or default. At the end of the life cycle, all the loans that have defaulted are counted, to calculate the long-run rate of default for the group.

When this procedure is repeated for successive groups of loans across a decade, a picture of the SBA program as a whole emerges (Figure 2.1). The picture shows that at the time of their maturity, default will have claimed 23.8 percent of five year loans, 24.6 percent of ten year loans, and various percentages of loans of other maturities. One year loans reach a much lower lifetime default rate, because they have short lives, in spite of their higher per period risk. The weighted average for the SBA program as a whole, 23.5 percent, reflects the preponderance of loans between five and ten years.

This same process is shown in tabular form (Table 2.2) for a representative group of 1,000 loans of seven year maturity. The first two columns show rates of purchase (conditional probabilities) and full repayment (early repayment) on an annualized basis. Each year the number of loans purchased and prepaid is estimated from the rates of purchase or prepayment, and these numbers are subtracted from the loans outstanding to yield the next year's outstanding loans. The final two columns cumulate the loans purchased and fully repaid. The final sums are the long-run rates. A total of 247 of the 1,000 seven year loans are purchased. Another 454 loans are fully paid before maturity, and, in the absence of further specific information, the final 299 loans are assumed to be paid in full at maturity, although it is known that a substantial portion will be paid late, and a few more will eventually default. Table 2.3 summarizes the results for different maturity groups, showing how many loans were in each group.

These rates are substantially higher than the published figures SBA presents, which were mentioned above. The default problem is worse than generally acknowledged. SBA does maintain its own estimate of the long-run rate of purchase, though this receives very limited circulation. As of the start of fiscal year 1983 it estimated 16.4 percent.[2] The method for calculating this figure is not explained. A still less widely circulated source, the evaluation of historical data by Estefania, produced a long-run rate of purchase of 20.7 percent, covering the years from 1969 to 1977.[3] The data came from the same SBA loan monitoring system as the data used here, and the approach to estimation was roughly similar, so it is not surprising that the results are also close.

Figure 2.1
Cumulative Purchases, as Loans Age (quarterly, by maturity group)

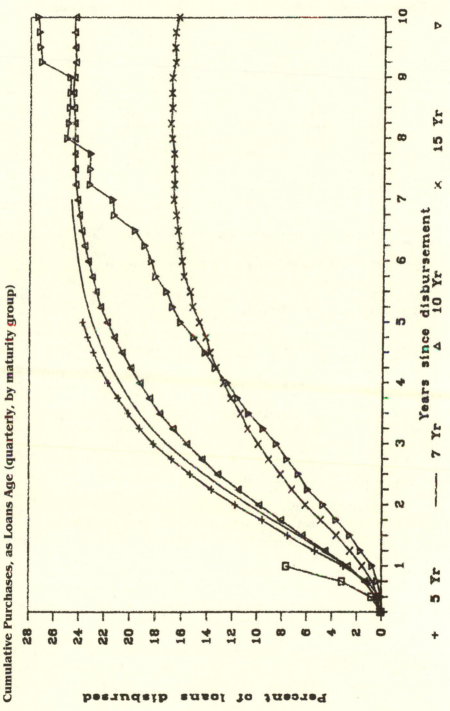

Table 2.2
Calculation of Long-Run Default and Prepayment Proportions
(representative portfolio of 1,000 seven year loans)

Loan Age	Probability of Purchase	Probability of Prepayment	Number of loans a/ Purchased	Number of loans a/ Prepaid	Cumulative Status Outstanding b/	Cumulative Status Purchased	Cumulative Status Prepaid
0	--	--	--	--	1,000	--	--
1	3.0%	1.2%	29	12	959	29	12
2	8.8%	5.5%	78	49	832	107	61
3	8.5%	8.3%	65	63	705	172	123
4	5.7%	11.6%	36	74	594	208	197
5	4.2%	16.1%	22	85	488	231	282
6	2.6%	19.3%	11	82	394	242	364
7	1.7%	27.2%	6	89	299 c/	247	454

a/ Conditional probabilities from first two columns, times loans outstanding in previous period.

b/ Number outstanding in previous period, less number purchased and prepaid in current period.

c/ It is assumed that all these loans are repaid at maturity.

Table 2.3
Rates of Purchase, by Maturity

Statistic	Weighted Average	----------- M a t u r i t y ----------- One	Five	Seven	Ten	Fift'n	Twenty
Number of loans	120,052	2,511	24,516	46,096	34,648	9,980	2,301
Percent of all loans	100.0%	2.1%	20.4%	38.4%	28.9%	8.3%	1.9%
Long run purchase rate a/	23.5%	7.7%	23.8%	24.7%	24.6%	16.8%	27.4%

a/ For fifteen and twenty year loans, purchase rate after ten years.

Age and Economic Condition Effects

Defaults do not occur at a steady rate throughout loan life cycles, which is one of the reasons the long-run rate is so hard to calculate. The probability of default is affected by various factors, chiefly loan age and external economic conditions.

When SBA loan purchases are viewed solely as function of the age of the loans, a very clear and predictable pattern emerges (Figure 2.2). The rate of default is small at first, but rises steadily to a peak near the end of the second year. It falls off gradually thereafter to a negligible level for loans that are still outstanding after seven years. Loans whose original maturity is five years or less tend to default sooner, and this pattern is strongest in the loans of shortest maturity, such as one year loans, which are not shown on the graph. After about the third or fourth year loans of

Figure 2.2
Propensity to Default by Age (quarterly probabilities, by maturity)

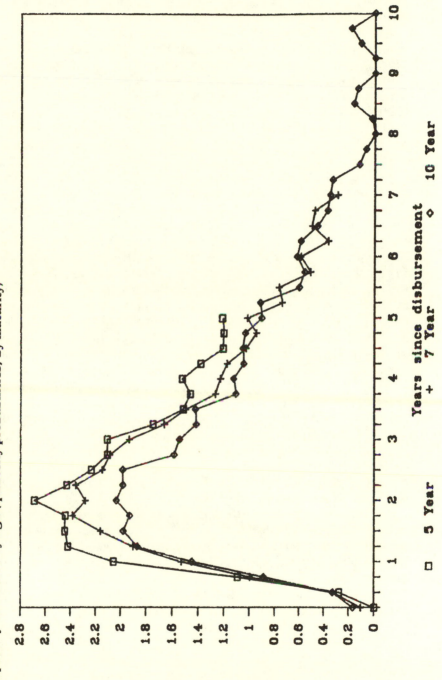

all maturities default at roughly the same low rates. Any bank needs to be aware of this pattern of change in order to predict cashflows.

The figure indicates the timing of the bank request to SBA for purchase. Another important indicator is the timing of borrower failure, the time at which regular repayments stop. Inspection of purchased loans indicates that this averages eight months before purchase. This is important for two reasons. First, it reveals more precisely the times when borrowers are most likely to fail. When borrower failure is at issue, the entire graph shown in Figure 2.2 can be shifted left by eight months. Second, it shows that banks wait far longer than the minimum two months before asking SBA to purchase the loans.

The age pattern gives clues to the nature of defaults. For example, it allows us to hypothesize about how borrowing businesses react to taking on a major debt. The pattern of purchases, adjusted to show the end of regular repayments, indicates that businesses face a critical testing period from about one-half year through two and a half years after borrowing. This conforms to what is known about how SBA loans are used. Most frequently, SBA loans finance a combination of fixed asset purchases and working capital. Initially, the working capital funds are likely to be available as a source of repayments. By the second and third year the investments made with the loan should have become the main source of funds for repayment. If these investments are not bringing in the expected income, or are taking too long to break even, the borrower runs short of cash. If the new assets prove able to generate income through these critical second and third years, the business is likely to be viable enough to continue to support the debt in later years. In addition, inflation may by that time have noticeably reduced the real cost of debt service for these fixed rate loans. This was true during the decade studied (1973–1983).

The incentives of the loan contract may contribute to the very low default probabilities seen in the later years. At the start of a loan's life, when little principal has been repaid, the funds owed are comparable to the value of the security that would be lost if the borrower defaulted. Later, when only a small amount remains outstanding, the prospect of losing the collateral may loom larger to the borrower than the difficulty of repaying the loan. This effect is well known among private home mortgages, and should apply to SBA loans as well, especially since many are secured by the business owners' personal real estate.

The pattern of default among SBA loans suggests an important conclusion about the riskiness of short- versus long-term lending, one which may apply to commercial lending generally. The analysis showed that loans of shorter maturity were more vulnerable to default at any given time than longer term loans. This is contrary to the conventional wisdom which considers longer term loans to be riskier, in large part because events in the more distant future that affect a borrower's ability to repay cannot be readily foreseen. The results shown here appear to contradict that premise in two ways. First, the shorter term loans are actually riskier. For any given period it is safer to hold a fifteen year SBA loan than a five year SBA loan. One year loans are by far the most default prone, month for month.

Second, and more fundamentally, most defaults occur during the second and third years after disbursement, well within the normal time horizon of most commercial banks. Unforseen risks of later years have been quite small throughout the decade, in comparison with near term risks. Most loans that default do so rather quickly. The first point could be explained away if it was guessed that lenders allot their longer term loans to safer borrowers, so that the difference represents bank judgment, rather than anything inherent in the term structure of loans. This would not affect the second point, however.

This finding should tell bankers something about credit risks of non-SBA commercial loans. There is no reason to suspect that the basic patterns of behavior for SBA and non-SBA loans would differ. While SBA loans default much more frequently, the age structure of non-SBA defaults should show the same humped pattern. If this does hold true for non-SBA loans, it suggests that banks could be more confident in making term loans, at least from the point of view of credit risk.

Why then are banks reluctant to make longer term loans? Interest rate and liquidity risk are two important factors. In addition, bankers may look not at their risk per unit of time, but rather at the total risk of individual loans. Very short term loans have a lower expectation of default over their lifetimes than intermediate and long term loans. However, if a banker views the portfolio as a whole, total expected defaults would be lower on a portfolio made up of longer term SBA loans than on one made up of short-term SBA loans. It would be worthwhile to collect and analyze data to see if the same holds true for non-SBA loans as well. In the meantime, banks may shun longer term loans because of interest rate or liquidity risk, but the evidence here suggests that they should not do so because of credit risk.

Age is not the only determinant of the rate of default among SBA loans; defaults are also strongly affected by the business cycle. In order to highlight this sensitivity to the economy, in Figure 2.3 the effect of age on default rates has been taken out, isolating the changes over calendar time. The probabilities shown in that figure are those that SBA would have experienced if the age mix of its portfolio had been static.

The first point of note is that there is no consistent trend toward a higher or lower level of default. This would indicate that the program itself neither improved nor deteriorated dramatically during the period from 1973 through 1983. In fact, if the results obtained by Estefania for an earlier period are considered, it can be concluded that there has not been a major change in long-run default rates, apart from the influence of the business

Figure 2.3
Propensity to Default, Calendar Period (quarterly, by maturity)

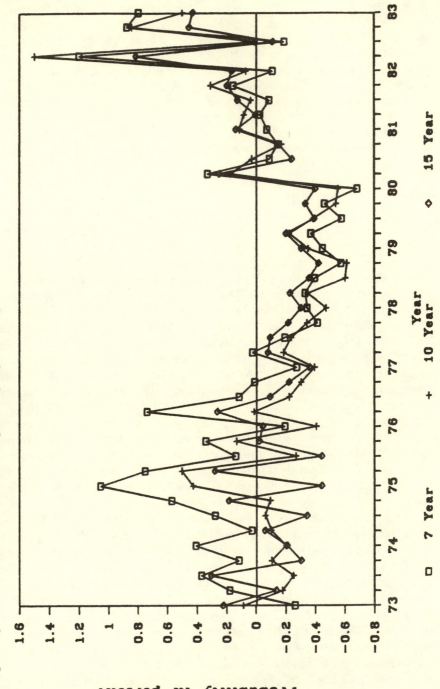

Table 2.4
Probability of Purchase by Calendar Period, Annualized (probability of purchase within one year)

Year	Weighted Average	One	Five	Maturity Seven	Ten	Fifteen	Twenty
1973	6.2	18.7	8.8	6.2	4.4	3.1	6.1
1974	7.7	29.1	13.7	7.1	4.4	2.6	7.6
1975	9.2	44.8	14.9	8.1	5.6	2.4	14.6
1976	7.0	38.9	10.0	6.4	3.9	2.9	12.9
1977	4.9	11.6	7.0	4.9	3.7	2.3	6.2
1978	3.7	4.1	4.9	4.1	2.8	1.7	3.2
1979	3.6	2.0	4.5	3.9	3.3	1.8	2.9
1980	4.7	5.0	5.3	5.2	4.3	2.5	2.7
1981	5.4	4.3	5.8	5.7	5.4	3.5	4.4
1982	6.9	5.4	6.7	7.5	7.3	4.3	3.6
Mean	5.9	16.39	8.16	5.91	4.51	2.70	6.42

cycle, from 1969 through 1983. Indications are that since 1983, no dramatic change has occurred.

This does not conflict with the graphically clear point that the variation from one year to the next in the default rate is substantial. From the best year, 1979, to the worst year, 1975, the weighted average default rate more than doubled (Table 2.4). Shorter term loans tend to vary more widely than longer ones, and are more likely to be purchased within any given year. If these monthly fluctuations in the probability of default are graphed against major macroeconomic variables, or analyzed using multiple regression, it becomes apparent that the changes follow the business cycle very closely. Defaults are much more likely to occur during recessions than during periods of economic growth. This can easily be seen if movement of the probabilities of purchase is plotted against changes in the index of industrial production (Figure 2.4), which is an indicator of the level of real activity in the economy. The simple conclusion is that the health of SBA guaranteed loans is highly dependent on whether the economy is growing. Industrial production explains 57 percent of the total variation in default rates for seven year loans in a regression. If combined with a time trend, this rises to 77 percent.

It is a significant, and somewhat surprising finding that several other key macroeconomic variables have relatively little to do with the default rate. Variables that have little explanatory power include the interest rate (real and nominal), the stock market index, inflation, and several variables relating to the performance of sectors in which SBA borrowers are concentrated, such as retail, wholesale, and services.

Probably the most surprising of these is the lack of importance of interest rates. There is a widespread belief that high interest rates (or credit ra-

Figure 2.4
Defaults versus Industrial Production (defaults are 6-month moving average)

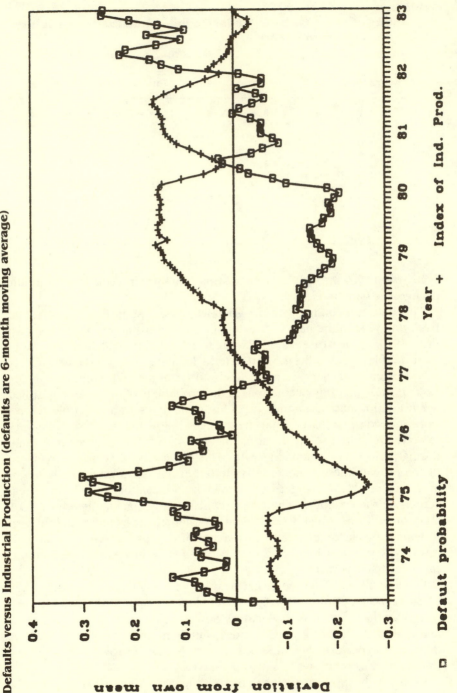

tioning associated with high rates) create severe problems for small business. This is not borne out by SBA defaults. To some extent, the borrowers of the SBA loans studied here were insulated from the effect of interest rate changes by their possession of long-term loans, particularly loans with fixed rates. (The great majority of SBA guaranteed loans are fixed rate. A small number of variable rate loans are made, but were not included in the data analyzed here.) Debt service on these SBA loans does not rise with the general level of interest rates, real or nominal, and the long maturity frees borrowers from having to seek financing from banks frequently. Protection would not be complete, however, because most SBA borrowers depend on substantial amounts of shorter term working capital credit, which would have to carry current rates.

In order to be sure that interest rates had little effect, the probabilities of default were examined during two time periods, before and after November 1979. The relationship between interest rates and the business cycle differed from the first to the last portion of the decade studied. During the first portion, 1973 through 1979, recession was associated generally with low interest rates. During the last three years, in contrast, a severe recession took place while interest rates remained high in real terms. It was hypothesized that this combination was particularly conducive to business failures, as businesses could not afford to borrow funds needed to sustain them through the slow sales period. For investigation of this hypothesis the decade was split into two parts to see if the interaction between business cycle indicators and interest rates differed significantly. The split separates October and November 1979, when the Federal Reserve changed its method of controlling the money supply, and higher, more volatile interest rates ensued. The results of this split differ little from those for the decade as a whole: industrial production is still the most important variable, and interest rates contribute little. The main lesson is that whatever effect high interest rates may have on small businesses in general, they do not cause holders of SBA loans to default, and are probably less important causes of business failure for all firms than is often thought. The ability of small firms to stay in business rests fundamentally on the level of demand in the economy. This basic relationship did not change during the decade.

The examination of the effect of economic conditions relates to, but does not resolve, a major question regarding the goals of the program. Some claim that a primary goal is to exert an economic stabilization effect. It is tempting to conclude on the basis of the wide fluctuations in default probabilities and their links to macroeconomic growth and recession, that the program exerts little or no countercyclical effect, at least not on existing borrowers. Holding an SBA loan does not exempt borrowers from vulnerability to recessions. The countercyclical question cannot be resolved, however, without a control group by which to judge what failure rates would have been in the absence of SBA loans, and this is not available here.

BEHAVIOR OF PURCHASED LOANS

Until now we have focused on purchase as the main indicator of default. Purchase served as a shorthand expression for default, an indicator of the number of SBA-guaranteed borrowers that experience severe trouble. But purchase is not a final outcome. Now we turn to the final disposition of the loans that are purchased. For these loans, charge off is the indicator of ultimate failure, and most purchased loans eventually require charge off.

After a loan is purchased its life cycle continues. Like nonperforming loans in the portfolio of any bank, the loans that SBA purchases usually retain some value. If it appears that the borrower will be able to make some regular payments, an amended loan agreement is negotiated, usually involving extension of maturity and occasionally reduction of the interest rate. If a borrower keeps the new schedule, the loan is removed from liquidation. Otherwise, assets are sold and losses are charged off. While some further repayments may come in, the main value remaining among charged off loans is the value recoverable through sale of collateral. The amount of principal finally charged off by SBA may range in value from virtually all of the original principal to very little.

The two final dispositions of purchased loans, full repayment and charge off, can be analyzed in much the same way that full repayment and purchases were viewed above, by following the progress of successive groups of loans, each purchased at the same time, until one or the other outcome occurs, and then calculating the long-run rate of charge off.

The results of such an analysis show that shortly after a group of SBA loans is purchased, a sizeable subset have become identifiable as hopeless cases, and these are charged off quickly. By the end of two years, two-fifths of all loans purchased will have been charged off. The rate at which charge offs occur then levels off, probably because borrowers that have not been charged off within two years have resumed some payments. By the end of ten years (the limit of our observation), 77 percent of all the originally purchased loans will have been charged off, and 16 percent will have recovered and repaid in full. Another 7 percent of the purchased loans will still be in SBA's hands. By extrapolation, it appears that most of these will eventually be charged off, for a final rate of charge off of 83 percent of all purchased loans. Working backwards, this means that 19.5 percent of all SBA loans are eventually charged off. A final summary of the year by year and final disposition of SBA-guaranteed loans is given in Table 2.5. The numbers shown in the table differ slightly from the SBA-wide average, because they are limited to seven year loans. They indicate

Table 2.5
Disposition of Loans after Seven Years (representative portfolio of 1,000 seven year loans)

YEAR	--------- E v e n t s ---------- Pur-chases	Prepay ments	Charge Offs	Recov-eries a/	---- F i n a l S t a t u s ---- Paid Fully b/	Charged Off	Bank Held c/	SBA Held
1	29	12	7	1	13	7	959	21
2	107	61	30	5	66	30	832	72
3	172	123	62	10	134	62	705	100
4	208	197	92	15	213	92	594	100
5	231	282	119	20	302	119	488	92
6	242	364	139	24	388	139	394	78
7	247	454	155	27	481	155	299 d/	65
Final	247	299	208	39	792	208	0	0

a/ Loans that are purchased and subsequently fully repaid.

b/ Sum of prepayments and recoveries.

c/ Loans neither purchased nor prepaid.

d/ All bank held loans outstanding after 7 years are assumed to be fully repaid.

that for a representative group of 1,000 seven year loans, 247 will default, 39 of these will recover, leaving 208 that will be charged off.

These percentages refer to the number of loans that fail. It is also important to note the amount of principal lost for these failing loans. On average, the outstanding portion of loans at the time of purchase is 86 percent of original principal, and at the time of charge off, the amount of principal recorded as a loss averages 86 percent of the amount purchased, or 74 percent of original principal. Thus, when an SBA loan goes bad, the amount of the loss is a very substantial portion of the original loan.

HOW MANY ARE TOO MANY?

The bottom line that is all too clear at this stage is that a quarter of all SBA-guaranteed borrowers are unable to repay their loans without major difficulty, and that most of those, a fifth of all SBA borrowers, never complete repayment. These numbers may strike some readers as high, others as reasonable. They struck the author as high enough to cause serious concern. The default figures lead one to ask: Should the U.S. government continue to sponsor a program that makes it a partner in failure for so many businesses?

The default rates cannot answer their own question without the introduction of additional information. The answer depends on one's perception of the purpose of the program. Program supporters cite two major rationales, and the information developed in the following chapters enables these to be assessed. One of the rationales for creating the SBA program is to correct for a presumed financial market failure that makes banks too risk averse regarding small business term loans. The standard implied by a properly functioning credit market is financial self-sufficiency because no private market would continue an operation that was not self-financing. Only if the government carries out the operation on a self-financing basis has it proved the private market wrong. Therefore, the only evidence required to determine whether this rationale is valid, is an assessment of the program's financial costs and revenues, which accrue to banks and SBA. The next two chapters will translate the default performance of SBA loans into financial flows received by lenders and SBA.

The second program rationale is that small businesses generate extra social and economic benefits that compensate for the added defaults. To determine whether this rationale is valid, a straightforward cost-benefit calculation could be performed, in which all the costs generated by the failed loans (to banks, borrowers, and SBA) would be balanced against all benefits generated by the successful loans. Unfortunately, this analysis is partially constrained by a lack of data. Costs to banks and SBA can be estimated rather thoroughly, with the help of the behavior model described above. However, costs to borrowers, and more importantly, benefits resulting from SBA loans, can only be guessed at. Very few studies have examined the impact of SBA loans on borrowers. In the absence of good information, we cannot resolve the social and economic benefit question, but we can frame it precisely enough to show the likely answer. By using costs and default rates as a base it is possible to show just how great the social and economic benefits of each successful SBA loan would have to be in order to compensate for the failures and their costs. Then we are left to speculate on whether, from all we know about them, SBA borrowers are likely to produce benefits of the required magnitude. In short, the answer to the question of how many defaults are too many depends on the financial costs of those defaults, and on the benefits produced by loans that do not default.

The next two chapters develop the evidence first on cost to banks, then on cost to SBA. The costs are estimated by attaching financial information to the behavior model described in this chapter. Chapter 5 examines the ultimate justifications for the program and makes assessments based on the models developed in Chapters 2 through 4. In the process of developing the information on costs, the next two chapters also produce a detailed description of the incentives and response to incentives that are built into the program. In particular, they highlight the importance of bank decision making on the key program parameters, including defaults, and in turn, place responsibility on SBA for setting proper incentives for banks. This description is, finally, as important as any yes or no conclusion on the current program's costs and benefits. It is not really possible to understand the SBA program without understanding the behavior of banks that use it. Such an understanding makes possible an assessment of the effect of changes in the program on the major players, and thereby leads to realistic proposals to improve the program's performance.

NOTES

1. Robert Morris Associates, *Annual Survey of Commercial Bank Loan Charge-Offs* (Philadelphia, 1980 and 1981), p. 9.

2. SBA, Office of Accounting Operations. "Memorandum on Fiscal Year 1982 Loss Rates," Unpublished, March 1983.

3. J. Ramon Estefania, "Financial Status of the SBA 7(a) Guaranty Program: Budgeting, Effects of the Economy on Losses and Alternatives to the Present Program," Internal SBA study, September 1980.

3 SBA Loans and Banks

Banks that participate in the SBA program intend to make money from it. By attaching cashflows to the loan life cycles described in Chapter 2 it is possible to assess whether or not they do.

The question of whether banks make a profit is one of the most hotly debated issues related to the SBA program. One view is that the program offers banks unusually high profits. For example, one article on the secondary market portion of the program claimed to show, "How the SBA condones profiteering by the banks."[1] According to this view, the guarantee protects banks from default costs to such a great degree that the loans become virtually the equivalent of government securities. Yet banks receive interest at levels up to 2 percent above the prime rate. Such rates could be fair for private loans because lenders need compensation for risks, but for loans with a 90 percent guarantee, some observers believe the rates exceed the appropriate level.

The main objection to high profits is that banks should not absorb the benefits meant for borrowers. Banks are not the intended beneficiaries of this program; they are solely agents for the government. Their role is to carry out the responsibilities SBA delegates to them for borrower selection and loan extension. Even if an aim of the program is to convince banks to favor small business lending, a subsidy to them would not be an appropriate way of doing so. Indeed, a subsidy would dissuade banks from developing their own, full-cost program of lending to such clients. The program should not give banks excess profits. If it does, it could probably be restructured to provide the same impact at lower cost.

A competing view, put forward largely by banks, is that the program offers returns that are too low. This view emphasizes the high administrative costs of SBA's paperwork requirements, and a default rate that results in high costs even after the guarantee. Evidence that banks take this point of view seriously is that relatively few banks participate actively in the program and that there appears to be relatively little pressure from banks for expanding the program's loan volume.

A third point of view, which might be termed the economists' view, is that competitive forces among banks could be expected to keep returns to banks at the minimum level required to induce them to participate. The return that banks would receive in a competitive financial market would fully compensate for their costs and risks, but assure them no added profit. If returns were lower, banks would lose money and stop making SBA loans, or alter their way of administering the loans to improve returns. On the other hand, if some banks received far more than the minimum, other banks would offer SBA loans at lower interest rates. The forces of interbank competition would drive returns toward the break-even level. This competitive level would also be the maximum that the SBA could offer without actually giving banks a subsidy.

The first half of this chapter attempts to determine which of these three points of view is most accurate by piecing together available information on the financial impact of the SBA program on banks, using the economist's definition of competitive returns. After a discussion of what is meant by a competitive return, the chapter presents the results of an assessment of returns, constructed by adding each major element of cost, revenue, and risk facing banks that make SBA loans, onto the model of the timing and frequency of loan defaults from the previous chapter.

When all the elements are combined, the returns to banks appear to be at or just below the competitive level. According to the evidence, banks are not absorbing a subsidy. Rather, an average SBA lender may receive a return that is slightly below the acceptable level.

In the second half of the chapter we pursue a number of investigations that seek to explain the result. If banks make a return that is slightly below the minimum, why do they participate in the SBA program at all? One answer may be that banks count their costs and returns differently from the way that they are counted here, which takes an average bank's costs into account. Some banks face lower administrative, default, or funds costs than those described here, and thus actually make a higher return on SBA loans. Lower costs could be due to the bank itself or could be achieved by the way it handles SBA loans, for example, by neglecting loan maintenance. Still other banks may make poor returns on individual SBA loans, but still value the program along other dimensions, for example, as a marketing device.

The observation that banks follow different strategies in making SBA loans leads one to ask what kind of banks participate. Analysis of data on the distribution of SBA loans by banks shows that not all banks participate, and those that do have different patterns of participation. These may coincide with different strategies for improving the value of SBA loans, as discussed in the last section of this chapter. SBA should consider which patterns of participation it wishes to encourage.

VALUE TO BANKS OF SBA LOANS

Definition of Competitive Returns

If financial markets are competitive, the base return expected on all financial investments will be equivalent, after the value of their particular features, costs, and risks have been accounted for. The ease with which financial assets are bought and sold, and actions by arbitragers tend to insure that financial markets do in general operate very competitively.

The competitive rate of return for any given investment, which appears as an effective interest rate, is a combination of three elements, the risk-free interest rate, risk premium, and explicit costs. The first element measures the time value of money, inflation, and expectations about future interest rates. It can be considered an economywide base interest rate. It is usually thought to be reflected in the interest rate on U.S. Treasury securities, which are freer from risks and costs than any other securities.[2] Risk, or unpredictable fluctuations in the future value of the asset, requires the second element, the risk premium. Risk is priced according to another economywide standard, which measures both the perception of how risky the economy as a whole is, and how risk averse the average investor is. This standard is usually estimated from returns required on the stock market. The third element accounts for direct costs associated with owning the asset. For bank loans this includes administrative expenses and expected losses due to default. As direct expenses on bank loans are far higher than the costs of owning a government security or a corporate bond, the competitive interest rate on bank loans will be higher.

The analytical importance of the competitive return is that it does not include any excess profit; it includes exactly enough compensation to induce investors to invest. The first two groups of critics of the SBA program should be willing to look at a competitive return as also a fair return: it is not subsidized, but it is enough.

The competitive return on an asset is calculated by setting its current value equal to the discounted value of the cashflows it will generate in the future. For a bond this means that price should equal the discounted value of its interest payments and ultimate redemption amount. For a bank loan it means original principal should equal monthly payments, less costs. In both cases, the discount rate should reflect the economy's base interest rate and any risk premium.

The procedure used in this case to assess whether the return is competitive is to insert the appropriate discount rate and solve for the present value. The present value of all revenues less costs is compared to the original loan amount (which has been standardized at one). If the calculation shows the discounted present value to equal the original loan amount (one), the loans will have been found to generate competitive returns for the banks. In other words, if the discounted present value equals one, the internal rate of return will have been found to equal the appropriate competitive rate.

Elements Determining Value to Banks

The information used to calculate the return to banks on SBA-guaranteed loans is based on the life cycle model of Chapter 2, with the addition of some further information specific to SBA and some information from the banking industry and economy in general. The cost and program information used is relevant to the decade from 1973 through 1983.

Interest Rate, Maturity, and Monthly Payment. Monthly average interest rates on SBA loans during the decade varied from a low of 8.3 percent in January 1973 to a high of 20.6 percent in October 1981 for seven year loans, with an average rate of 12.4 percent.[3] Rates for other maturities varied through similar ranges. These interest rates together with maturities are sufficient to generate a monthly amortization schedule and expected cashflows for the portfolio.

Frequency of Default and Prepayment and Amount of Loss. The life cycle model of Chapter 2 contains all the information necessary to calculate the deviations of loans from their prescribed schedules, and the timing and frequency of defaults and early repayments. Additional analysis of the same data yields information on the value to banks of loans that default.

Administrative Expenses. The administrative costs of SBA loans include bank staff salaries, physical overhead, and services contracted, such as property appraisal. The little available information on such costs is scattered. Banks commonly believe SBA loans cost them more to administer than do similar unguaranteed loans, because of SBA's paperwork requirements, and extra management assistance needed by SBA's less established type of borrowers. On the other hand, SBA loans tend to be longer term and larger than most bank loans, which provides a larger base over which to prorate high initial costs. In the absence of specific data on SBA, the next best source is data on the costs of private commercial loans published by the Federal Reserve Board in its annual *Functional Cost Analysis,* compiled through surveys of banks nationwide. To estimate SBA costs, the *Functional Cost Analysis* figures are adjusted upwards by 10 percent on the basis of an informal survey of bankers actively involved in the SBA program. However, SBA lenders receive an initial 1 percent guarantee fee, which offsets some of the costs.[4]

Discount Rate. The seven year Treasury bond rate is used as the risk-free discount rate. The spread between the interest rate and the discount rate supplies the margin from which default losses and administrative costs must be covered. The spread during the decade ranged from 1.5 percent to 7.3 percent, averaging 3 percent (Figure 3.1).

After extensive analysis of the variation in expected returns on portfolios of SBA loans, it can be shown that no additional premium need be added to the discount rate to compensate for risk. While this may at first appear counterintuitive, the explanations are simple. First, the losses due to default can be predicted and treated as a cost rather than an uncertainty, and second, the effect of the guarantee is to reduce the actual variation in return banks experience to a negligible amount. SBA loans may go to risky businesses, but because loan losses are limited and can be accurately forecast, a pool of SBA loans is not a risky asset for a bank to hold. (See Appendix for further discussion of risk in SBA loans.)

Present Values of SBA Loans

When all the cost and revenue elements are assembled and set at their average levels for the decade, the estimated present value to banks of the SBA portfolio is on average just below the break-even level (Table 3.1). The present values of longer maturity loans are slightly higher than average, reflecting an assumption that there are no defaults in the later years of the loans' lives, after our 123 month observation period has ended. One and five year loans offer lower returns because they retain little value in case of default. The weighted average present value for all maturities is 0.99. If the same portfolio of loans received no bank guarantee (and involved no guarantee fee), its value would be 0.90. Because of the assumptions used to generate these estimates, there is some uncertainty surrounding them. We cannot conclusively state that the guaranteed value calculated is significantly different from the break-even level. An appropriate statement of the findings, taking this uncertainty into account, is that the returns on SBA loans are at or slightly below the break-even level, or that for every dollar of loan principal banks extend, the estimate shows them to receive a discounted net cashflow worth 99 cents to a dollar in present value terms. The cost- and risk-adjusted return on SBA loans is near the return on other investments such as corporate bonds or government securities adjusted according to the same principles.

This finding answers one of the central questions in evaluating the performance of the SBA program. Banks are not, on average, using this program to achieve unusually high profits. The interest rate they receive and the protection from loss afforded by the guarantee barely offset the costs of default, administration, and a minimum discount rate. Concerns that banks are "profiteering" through this program can be safely set aside.

Rather, a central question becomes the following. If banks receive a

Figure 3.1
SBA and Treasury Interest Rates (seven year maturities, quarterly)

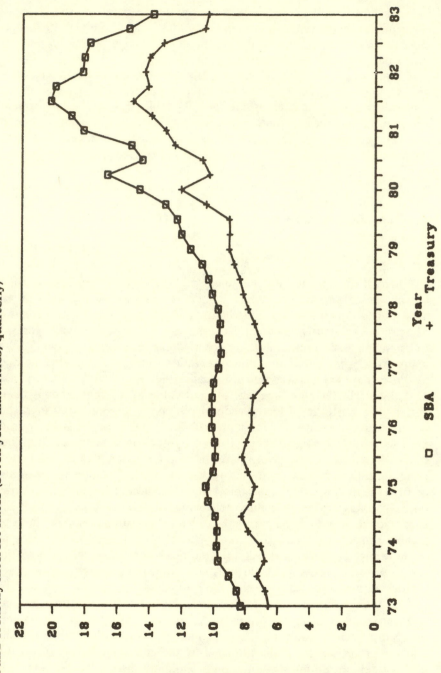

Table 3.1
Present Values of SBA Loans [a]

Maturity	Banks	Unguaranteed Total
One year	0.971	0.953
Five years	0.982	0.883
Seven years	0.989	0.893
Ten years	0.993	0.908
Fifteen years	1.006	0.963
Twenty years	1.007	0.954
Weighted average	0.990	0.904

a/ Assumes all cost elements are at
   average for decade.

minimal return on SBA loans, why do they participate in the program? The possible answers to this question are the main subject of the rest of this chapter, and are answered in two phases.

WHY BANKS PARTICIPATE: TWO APPROACHES

The first step in examining the question is to observe that any given bank may not receive the 99 cents on its SBA portfolio estimated here. One reason for this is that two of the assumptions used to calculate the estimate were taken from the economy at large rather than from banks that actually make SBA loans. The discount rate used was the societywide time value of money. It was adopted because of its wide validity as a way to compare one type of investment with others. However, banks would use some measure of their cost of funds as a discount rate in valuing the loans. Administrative costs were also taken from aggregate data covering all banks, not only those active in the SBA program. If the cost of funds or the administrative cost for those banks which actually make SBA loans are lower than the rates applied here, then the true return on the program is higher than calculated.

Even for a bank whose costs were at the average level, its return would still depend on the particular way it handles SBA loans. Bank decisions on how to run the SBA program could alter administration and funds costs and the interest rate. The changes would result from several possible strategies banks may adopt to increase the program's profitability. Some of these strategies are more successful for banks than others. More importantly, the strategies banks choose may have an impact on how well the SBA program performs.

The second approach to understanding why banks participate is to note that not all banks do. Only 17 percent of all banks held portfolios of more than ten SBA loans during the early 1980s, and presumably they were able to run the program more profitably than could the average bank. This chapter presents data on the distribution of SBA loans according to bank characteristics. From this information, insight can be gained into which banks participate and what their motivations might be.

First Approach: Strategies for Improving Profits

Each of the elements of costs and returns to banks contributes to the overall present value of the loans, though not equally. Some elements make a greater difference than others, and the crucial point for banks is that some elements are more amenable to change than others. By systematically varying one or more of these elements, as estimated in the model, while holding the rest of the model constant, it is possible to see how much potential a bank would have for increasing profits through changing the components of cost.

The structure of costs is given in Table 3.2, which shows the total contribution of each major component to final returns. The top line shows the present value as estimated. The remaining lines show the change that would occur if each element were reduced to zero. For example, if there were no defaults, the present value of seven year loans to banks would be the current value plus 0.02, or 1.01. The important message of these figures is that the present value to banks is far more dependent on administrative costs and interest rate spreads than on default rates.

The relative importance of components would be different without the guarantee. If there were no guarantee, the return on this portfolio would be dominated by defaults, and the interest rate spread would be unable to make up for the large losses.

The returns banks receive on SBA loans after the guarantee are surprisingly similar to those that would be received on a private, nonguaranteed portfolio. The table shows the present value components of a hypothetical private portfolio of seven year loans, using the actual costs given in Federal Reserve data, at decade averages. Default costs actually experienced by private banks are very close to those produced by SBA loans, after the guarantee has been taken into account. However, in order for a portfolio to produce default losses of this size without a guarantee, private bank loans would default about one tenth as often as SBA loans (assuming the value of a loan that defaults is the same in either case). SBA

Table 3.2
Contribution to Present Value of Cost and Receipt Components (seven year loans [a])

| | --- SBA Loans --- | | Private |
	Banks	Total b/	Loans c/
Present value under average conditions:			
	0.989	0.893	1.013
Effect of defaults on present value:			
	-0.018	-0.124	-0.013
Effect of administrative costs, including 1 percent fee:			
	-0.067	-0.062	-0.064
Effect of interest rate spread:			
	0.077	0.074	0.089

Sources: private loans, Functional Cost Analysis and Survey of Terms of Lending, Federal Reserve Board, SBA loans, author's calculations.

a/ Change in present value of loans if cost/receipt element were zero.

b/ Value of SBA portfolio if loans were unguaranteed. Total revenues produced by borrowers.

c/ Value of private seven year loans, assuming: default costs 0.3% per year, acquisition cost 1.7%, maintenance 1.14% per year, interest 12.48%.

loans are ten times more likely to default than private ones, according to this calculation.

Administrative costs would also be very similar to the SBA level. Although the SBA calculation assumes administrative costs to be 10 percent higher than for private loans, the contribution of administrative costs to the present value is slightly higher for private loans because fewer of the loans default, and therefore more remain outstanding until maturity. The interest rate spreads are also similar, because interest rate averages are almost identical for private and SBA loans (12.5 percent for private, 12.4 percent for SBA seven year). We now consider how banks could alter each component of cost and revenue to achieve higher profits.

Administrative Costs. Any bank could reduce the effective administrative cost of SBA loans by treating them as marginal activities. Under this

Table 3.3
Value of SBA Loans with Changes in Costs (seven year loans)

Change In Costs	--- To Banks ---- Value	Change	---- To SBA ---- Value	Change
Current level	0.989	--	-0.096	--
1. Acquistion and maintenance costs:				
Half current level	1.025	0.036	-0.096	--
2. Maintenance costs:				
Half current level	1.011	0.022	-0.096	--
Halved, defaults up 20%	1.007	0.018	-0.114	-0.018
Halved, defaults doubled	0.993	0.004	-0.179	-0.083
3. Default rate:				
No Defaults	1.007	0.018	0.000	0.096
Half current level	0.997	0.008	-0.046	0.050
Twice current level	0.981	-0.008	-0.140	-0.044
4. Collateral:				
Half current level	0.987	-0.002	-0.112	-0.016
Twice current level	0.990	0.001	-0.082	0.014
5. Cost of funds:				
CD rate	0.982	-0.007	-0.096	--
Average cost	1.091	0.102	-0.096	--
6. Interest rate				
Plus 25 basis points	0.995	0.006	-0.096	--
Plus 50 basis points	1.002	0.013	-0.096	--

strategy, SBA loans would only be made during times when there was an excess of administrative staff, as a way of making efficient use of resources for which the costs had already been incurred. In such cases, the marginal administrative cost assigned to SBA loans would be very low. Thinking of SBA loans in this way would make returns appear significantly more attractive. For example, if administrative costs were half of the amount we estimated, the present value of the loans to a bank would increase by 0.04 (Table 3.3, case 1). Of course any of a bank's loan could be regarded as its marginal activity, but it is more likely that SBA loans would be last in line, as they are given to the less promising of the loan applicants a bank sees.

A more obvious strategy would be for a bank to lower the administrative costs of SBA loans simply through neglect. Presumably this would somewhat increase the probability of default among borrowers. However, because of the damping effect of the guarantee, a bank could improve the profits it receives from the program by this strategy, despite even significantly increased defaults. We do not know the relationship between administrative efforts and defaults, but we can see that the linkage would have to be improbably strong before it would be worthwhile to spend more on administration as a way to reduce default costs. If a bank managed to halve ongoing loan maintenance costs (leaving initial costs the same), such as by overloading loan officers and dispensing with site visits, it would increase the present value of a portfolio of SBA loans by 2.2 percent (Table 3.3, case 2). Not unless defaults more than doubled would default costs use up this savings. If neglect made only a 20 percent increase in default probabilities, banks would still be 1.8 percent ahead. A bit of anecdotal evidence that indicates banks actually follow such a strategy is the frequent complaint that banks assign their most junior, lowest salaried loan officers to SBA loans, using it in effect as a loan officer training program.

Default Costs. In contrast to strategies lowering administrative costs, strategies involving a reduction in the rate or cost of default would be unproductive. A bank could decrease the default rate among its borrowers by taking on only safer businesses. Because of the protection offered by the guarantee, this would profit a bank little, especially if it is administratively costly to improve borrower selection. If a bank were to decrease the default probability of a group of seven year SBA loans by half through more careful selection, the present value of the portfolio would change from .989 to .997, an increase of only .008 (Table 3.3, case 3). Conversely, a doubling of the default rate would only reduce its return by .008. This could be made up by a 30 basis point increase in the interest rate. If finding a doubly safe group of borrowers would require additional marketing efforts, a bank would face little motivation to try.

The picture is even more striking for a bank strategy involving lending to borrowers with poor collateral, or extending larger loans than would otherwise be allowed, given the value of collateral. A change in collateral coverage would directly change the value of a charged off loan, but because not all defaulting loans are charged off, it would have less impact on the overall value of purchased loans, and even less on the portfolio as a whole. A 50 percent increase or decrease in the value of charged off loans would lead to a 1.0 percent increase or decrease in the value of purchased loans to a bank, and a change of .002 in the portfolio present value (Table 3.3, case 4). There is surely little incentive for banks to verify the adequacy of collateral coverage for SBA loans.

Cost of Funds. The marginal cost of funds a bank would apply to SBA loans would reflect its cost of raising funds by means other than routine deposits, such as by selling certificates of deposit (CDs). It is unlikely that a bank would be able to show increased profits for SBA loans by using its marginal cost of funds rather than the government bond rate used here. The CD rate for the largest money center banks was very close to the government rate throughout the decade. The average CD rate was 26 basis points above the average Treasury rate on seven year bonds. Any bank using this CD rate as its cost of funds would show a slightly lower profitability from SBA loans (Table 3.3, case 5). Most banks would have to use a still higher rate; even large regional banks face higher premiums than the money center banks when they borrow by selling jumbo CDs.

The smallest banks, however, may use a far lower cost of funds rate because they may not contemplate raising funds through money markets. Many smaller banks, especially in rural areas, have relied on deposits alone to supply their funds. Throughout almost all of the period studied, interest on deposits was regulated. The marginal cost of funds for nonborrowing banks was therefore close to the average rate, which is recorded in the *Functional Cost Analysis*. The average spread throughout the decade between the average rate and the SBA lending rate was 6.7 percent. Any bank using such a fund-raising practice would calculate the return on SBA loans as 1.091. It should be noted, however, that as the funds cost is applicable to all bank loans, a bank using a low funds cost would give no special advantage to SBA loans relative to other loans. Differences in funds costs cannot be considered a strategy for increasing the profitability of the program, only an explanation of why SBA loans may meet minimum profit requirements for many banks.

Interest Rates. The easiest way for banks to increase profits on SBA loans would appear to be to raise interest rates, as long as increases were modest enough for customers to be willing to pay. An increase in the rate charged SBA borrowers of 25 basis points would raise the present value of the loans by .006, and an increase of 50 basis points would raise it by .013, to 1.002 (Table 3.3, case 6). Presumably, either of these changes would be easy to effect. It is not clear why banks do not charge SBA loans slightly higher interest rates. The rates they have charged have been very close to those on comparable commercial and industrial term loans made privately (Figure 3.2). Some of the restraint has come from the ceiling on SBA rates, which is usually a fixed percentage above the prime rate for loans of up to seven year maturity. However, the actual average rate has averaged at least 50 basis points below the ceiling, showing that some of the restraint comes from competitive forces. In particular, bankers are known to be reluctant to lend at higher rates when faced with higher cost borrowers, preferring instead to deny credit. Banks may wish to avoid being labeled as institutions that charge high rates.

The need for a ceiling on SBA interest rates is open to contest, at least on average. More often than not, banks charge below the ceiling. A ceiling may be desired as a way to protect borrowers against a minority of unscrupulous lenders. If such protection is desired, it would at a minimum be better to revise the basis for setting the ceiling. The ceiling has always been set in relation to the prime rate, a short-term rate. However, the rates actually charged on SBA loans vary much more closely with longer term rates, in keeping with their own maturities (see Figure 3.3 in comparison to Figure 3.1). If SBA rates follow longer term rates, there is a possibility that SBA loans will be squeezed out of the market during times

Figure 3.2
SBA and Private Loan Interest Rates (private, selected weeks; SBA, quarterly)

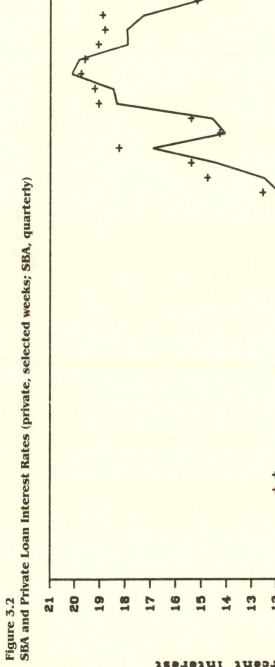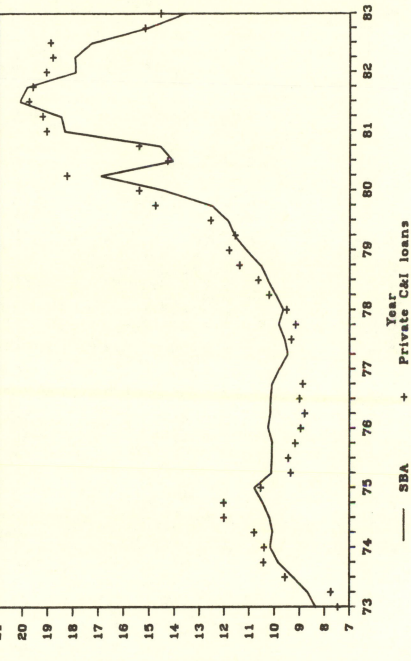

Figure 3.3
SBA and Prime Interest Rates (SBA seven year maturities, quarterly)

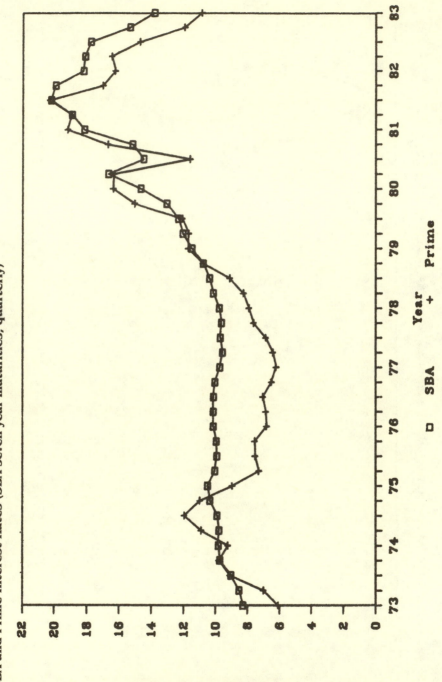

when short-term rates are further than usual below long-term rates, and banks will not make SBA loans. To avoid such an unnecessary problem, SBA should tie its ceiling to a longer term rate, such as that on five or seven year Treasury bills.

Customer Development. Many banks use the SBA loan program as a marketing tool. In a survey of bank participation in the SBA program, banks cited the ability to make loans to new businesses as one of the most important reasons for their participation. Among SBA borrowers, 25 percent are new firms, and an unknown number are firms that are new to the bank as borrowing customers, even if they are existing firms. The SBA program allows a bank to try out unknown borrowers. If the borrower defaults, the bank has lost very little. If the borrower proves successful, a permanent banking relationship can develop, involving deposits, fee services, short-term loans, and renewed longer term loans. Developing such relationships is an important objective of banks and also of the SBA program. Moreover, SBA loans allow banks to offer a given borrower longer maturities and larger loans, and can therefore be a means of attracting clients who might otherwise be served by other banks. The prospect of identifying new clients that can subsequently become ongoing customers could overcome weak expected returns on initial loans made with the guarantee.

Special Portfolio Benefits. SBA loans are given certain privileges that make them more attractive members of a bank's asset portfolio than ordinary business loans. The guaranteed portion is not counted as a loan by bank examiners in computing the various liquidity and capital adequacy ratios. This allows banks to extend their capital and deposit bases slightly farther, if they desire. SBA loans are also acceptable as collateral for federal reserve advances and government deposits. Another benefit, affecting only smaller participants, is that the guaranteed portion of SBA loans is not counted as part of the 10 percent of assets that can be lent to any single borrower. According to most surveys of bank attitudes to the SBA program, these special provisions are only important to a few of the banks who make SBA loans. Most banks claim that they are not pushing against their lending limits, and that the advantage of using SBA loans as public collateral is small, given that there are many other instruments acceptable for the same purpose. The most important of the special benefits afforded SBA loans is the ability to sell the loans to other investors through SBA's secondary market program, which will be discussed at length in a later chapter.

Second Approach: Which Banks Participate?

Although there are a variety of possible approaches to increasing the profitability of the SBA program, not all banks are able to find one that is useful for them. Among the most convincing evidence that on average the SBA program does not offer especially high returns is that not all banks participate, and of those that do, not all participate actively. A look at what types of banks participate a little, actively, or intensively can shed some light on which of the strategies reviewed here are most likely to be used.

There is no average bank user of SBA, but rather a wide variety of bank sizes and at each bank size, a wide range of levels of participation. This diversity shows that banks have many different reasons for making SBA loans. Most banks adopt one of four basic stances toward the program. The groups of banks that have chosen each of these four stances have different characteristics, and each group is likely to perform differently with respect to SBA's goals. SBA should consider which groups and which stances it wishes to encourage. By doing so it could have a significant impact on program performance.

SBA provided information on the number and dollar amount of SBA loans held by each bank in four states—Arkansas, Colorado, Massachusetts and Michigan—in February 1982. This distribution was compared with basic balance sheet information reported by each bank to the Federal Deposit Insurance Corporation three months earlier, for December 1981. The four states chosen represent different regions of the country, and the size and concentrations of their banking industries differ. Averages for the combination of all four are close to national averages for the SBA program. They are treated here as a single sample, assumed to be representative of the whole country.[5]

In the four states studied, about 72 percent of all commercial banks use the SBA program, that is, have at least one SBA loan in their portfolios. Nationwide, the percentage SBA reports is about the same, meaning that more than 10,000 banks of roughly 15,000 participate. The total number of SBA loans is not very large by comparison to the number of banks, so SBA loans tend to be spread very thinly (Table 3.4). The mean number of loans per participating bank is nine. Though there are a large number of very low participation banks, they account for a small portion of all the SBA loans. For example, the 21 percent of banks that hold only one or two loans account for only 7 percent of all loans. Most loans are held by more active participants in the program. Only 6 percent of all banks hold more than 20 loans, yet this 6 percent accounts for 40 percent of the SBA total.

SBA loans are widely distributed across banks of all sizes. Smaller banks have fewer SBA loans in their portfolios than large banks; however, SBA loans are relatively more important to them. For banks of $25 to $50 million in assets, SBA loans account for 1.3 percent of assets, while for banks over $500 million they account for only 0.3 percent. At the same time, virtually all the banks that opt out of the program are small (90 percent are smaller

Table 3.4
Groupings of SBA Loans in Banks [a]

Number of SBA Loans In Bank	---- B a n k s ----		----- L o a n s -----	
	Number	Percent	Number	Percent
0	313	28	0	0
1-2	232	21	490	7
3-5	202	18	630	9
6-10	171	15	1,330	19
11-20	123	11	1,820	26
21-50	58	5	1,610	23
Over 50	16	1	1,190	17
Total	1,115	100	7,000	100

Sources: SBA Lender Relations Division and FDIC Annual Report of Income and Condition.

a/ For Arkansas, Colorado, Massachusetts, Michigan.

than $50 million in assets), while almost every one of the largest banks participate. Such generalizations are not especially useful, however, because at every bank asset size the intensity of participation varies greatly from bank to bank. Asset size explains only 26 percent of the total variation in SBA portfolio size. Apparently, the choice of whether to participate in the SBA program is made on grounds highly specific to each bank.

The four participation types that banks fall into are (1) nonparticipants, (2) infrequent users (banks with less than 10 SBA loans), (3) active users (banks with at least 10 SBA loans, whose commercial and industrial (C & I) portfolios are less than 20 percent SBA loans), and (4) intensive users (at least 10 SBA loans; SBA loans at least 20 percent of C&I portfolios). Each of the groups differs strikingly from the others in characteristics such as asset size, capital adequacy, liquidity, rate of return, and loan losses (Table 3.5). Differences in the average characteristics of banks in each group help reveal their reasons for using SBA loans.

Nonusers

Over a quarter of all banks have no SBA loans, most of them very small and many in rural areas. They tend to be conservative in their lending policies, maintaining low loan to equity ratios, suffering few loan losses, and receiving a slightly lower return on equity than the average for all banks. Lack of participation may result from lack of knowledge about the program, or it may result from a decision that SBA loans are not profitable. SBA has heard complaints from banks who say that they are ending par-

Table 3.5
Groupings of Banks by SBA Participation [a]

Characteristics	All Banks	Non-Users	Infrequent Users	Active Users	Intensive Users
Number of banks	1106	305	582	158	58
Percent of banks	100	28	53	14	5
SBA Loans:					
Number (avg)	6.4	0	3.7	21.7	23.8
Amount (Thousands)	$699	$0	$407	$2,250	$3,005
Average loan size	$109	$0	$110	$104	$126
Percent of all SBA	100	0	31	46	23
SBA as percent of C&I	12	0	14	8	43
Bank characteristics:					
Assets (millions)	$105	$30	$53	$462	$52
Capital adequacy b/	0.87	0.60	1.00	1.28	1.19
Loans to equity ratio	6.7	5.4	6.7	8.6	7.5
Liquidity ratio	0.58	0.52	0.59	0.63	0.63
Return on equity	0.11	0.10	0.11	0.14	0.14
Loan losses to revenue	0.25	0.13	0.28	0.42	1.20

a/ In four states, Arkansas, Colorado, Massachusetts and Michigan.

b/ Capital adequacy is (medium term governments*0.04+long term governments*0.06+loans and other assets*0.1+real estate*0.5+ premises)/equity.

ticipation because of dissatisfaction with the program. The low return calculated above shows that such complaints may be valid for many banks.

Infrequent Users (less than 10 SBA loans)

Over half of all banks have between one and nine SBA loans. Although each bank holds few loans, SBA cannot neglect this group of banks, because they extend a third of all SBA loans. In most characteristics, these banks cannot be distinguished significantly from the average for all banks, though they include few of the really large banks.

Participation in SBA at such low levels cannot be viewed as part of a deliberate banking strategy. The reasons for participation are probably ad hoc: a particular borrower seeks the bank's loan after discussions with SBA, or a bank tries the program but never makes it part of regular bank policy. Such banks may make a minimum number to be able to claim community involvement. One official of a low participation bank reported that SBA loans were given only when there was pressure from some source, such as from a member of the bank's board of directors, to lend to a specific borrower.

Such banks are likely to take advantage of the incentives described above to be lax in borrower selection and follow up, and may give loans of larger size than otherwise warranted or with less collateral backing. Given the ad hoc reasons for participating, these banks may not care whether they make a profit from SBA loans. This would clearly be the case if they perceived them as the most effective way to respond to certain external pressures. The number of loans they have may be too small for them to know whether they run the program profitably. They may simply take the guarantee as an assurance that profits will come. If SBA loans are marginal activities, they may be squeezed in among other administrative duties, not adding directly to costs.

One would hypothesize that for all these reasons, defaults among this group would be higher than the SBA average, and data from the mid–1980s suggests that this is the case. Moreover, this group would not be using SBA loans to develop expertise in term lending to small firms, which would mean both that SBA could not be sure of the judgments the banks make on SBA loans, and that involvement in the program would produce no lasting changes in bank lending practices. If these hypotheses are correct, it would serve SBA's interests to discourage participation on this scale, or to encourage it only as a way to develop new active lenders. If it did so, the number of banks SBA would have to deal with would be greatly reduced, as this group accounted for three-quarters of all participating banks in 1982. This could have an additional benefit of reducing SBA's administrative costs.

Active Users (10 or more SBA loans, C&I portfolios less than 20 percent SBA loans)

The active users include many moderate sized banks and almost all the largest banks. Their average asset level is over four times as high as the average for all banks. They hold almost half of all SBA loans, but because of their size, the SBA loans are only a small proportion of their total assets.

Active bank participation in SBA is clearly deliberate. In many cases the size of the SBA portfolios is sufficient for staff members or departments to be devoted specifically to SBA. Such banks would have developed some procedures and guidelines for handling SBA loans. If participation in SBA has become a deliberate part of these banks' activities, it is very likely that some attention is paid to the profit associated with participation. Even if the primary motivation were fulfillment of community support obligations, profit would be considered. Such a bank would have few strategies for improving profits from the SBA program, however. It could not regard the administrative costs as incidental, nor is it likely to adopt a deliberate strategy of saving on administration while letting default rates rise. The likely ways of improving program performance would be to make loans with lower probabilities of default, to administer the program efficiently, and to charge slightly higher interest rates. Experience with the program would provide both the expertise and the information on past performance necessary to pursue such a strategy.

Although there is no data available to confirm this hypothesis directly, there is one piece of evidence to indicate that these banks pursue a more conservative policy for SBA loans. The average size of loans they make is smaller than the program average.

The hypothesis is that active users manage SBA portfolios effectively, and probably at below average default rates. If this is true (and SBA has data sufficient to verify whether it is), SBA should concentrate its guaranteed loans among them. It is already making such a move, in its certified and preferred lenders programs which are discussed in Chapter 6.

Intensive Users (at least 10 SBA loans, C&I loans over 20 percent SBA-guaranteed)

The last category of users is in many ways the most interesting. There are only a few banks that use SBA intensively, 5 percent in this sample. They extend 23 percent of all SBA loans, a significant proportion of the total. A mean of 43 percent of all their C&I loans are backed by SBA, which would probably mean that almost all term loans (over one year) are SBA guaranteed. For these banks, the SBA program is a major aspect of total financial operations. Banks in this category are often singled out to be used as examples of banks making excess profits from the program.

These banks have distinctive characteristics. They are about the same size as the infrequent users, fairly small, but their portfolio attributes resemble the large banks. The larger banks are able to extend more loans from the same equity base than can smaller banks and to cut their liquidity reserves slightly closer, for various reasons such as greater ability to diversify and fuller participation in money markets. This can be seen in the statistics of the active users compared with average banks or nonusers (capitalization, loan to equity ratio, liquidity ratio).

The intensive users pursue a highly leveraged strategy similar to those of the large banks, with high loan to equity ratios, low liquidity, and high returns on equity. Their most striking characteristic is a very high average loan loss rate. Given the importance of SBA loans to these banks, it is likely that the program is a part of the strategy that allows these banks to lend so aggressively.

The special characteristics of SBA loans allow them to be used in this way, including noncounting in liquidity and capital adequacy ratios, use as collateral for U.S. Treasury deposits and Federal Reserve advances, and the secondary market. Large active users would need none of these special benefits, both because they have other ways of achieving the same ends and because SBA loans are too small a portion of their total activity to make a noticeable difference. But the benefits could be crucial for smaller banks lacking alternatives.

Use of SBA loans as a strategy for faster growth would lead these banks to take on borrowers other banks would not serve, in order to reach new clients with little effort. If these loans were riskier, the guarantee would give protection. They might also offer more generous loan terms to existing clients of other banks in order to lure them away.

It is not clear what effect such actions would have on default rates, though they may involve higher than average ones. The intensive user banks have high loan loss rates for their private portfolios, which reveal a tolerance for higher rates of default generally. These banks also make larger than average SBA loans, another indication that risk may be greater. As shown above, the banks could offset higher defaults by lower administrative costs or higher interest rates.

If this hypothesis is correct, and these banks are using SBA as a bank development program, SBA should watch carefully for such banks, and monitor their default performance closely. If they perform well, they would be developing the kind of small business expertise SBA wishes to promote. If they perform poorly, SBA could minimize the potential negative effects by requiring banks to maintain a good record on defaults in order to continue to participate.

SBA would do well to find out whether the hypotheses about these four patterns of participation are correct by assembling data on SBA loan defaults, interest rates charged, and use of the secondary market by each category of bank. It has such information readily, though not publicly, available. This information could be used to concentrate SBA lending among the most efficient, responsible banks, and to encourage other banks to become more responsible. The certified and preferred lender programs, discussed in Chapter 6, are based on this notion.

NOTES

1. Harold Bergen, "The Maverick Moneylender," *The New Republic*, February 10, 1982, p. 21.

2. The yield curve, which sets different rates for different maturities is a part of this base rate. There are really a number of different base rates, one for each maturity.

3. These are the actual interest rates on the 120,000 loans analyzed in Chapter 2.

4. In 1986, the fee was raised to 2 percent.

5. A small proportion of SBA loans are made by nonbank lenders, including credit unions, savings and loan associations, finance companies, and public industrial development companies. A few of these nonbank lenders are among the most active of all SBA lenders. For consistency in drawing inferences, however, this analysis is strictly limited to banks.

4 Subsidies and Incentives

The focus broadens in this chapter to include SBA itself as the third player in the loan guarantee program, along with banks and borrowers. In administering the program, SBA is charged with making sure that the program achieves its ultimate purposes. In bearing the final program cost, SBA embodies the interests of the federal government, or more generally, taxpayers. Thus, for evaluating SBA's role in the program, the key questions involve the costs SBA bears and the effect on the program of SBA's policies. Now the inquiry deepens, and we begin to ask how the program might perform if its ground rules were changed.

At the center of this inquiry is the relationship between SBA and banks acting as their agents. SBA is concerned with the outcome of the program in terms first of its own financial cost and second of the achievement of the program's underlying economic and social goals. Yet, SBA cannot determine these outcomes directly. They are filtered through the decision-making apparatus of banks. SBA delegates responsibility to banks for making the central choices (borrower selection) and for day-to-day management (loan servicing). Banks will carry out these responsibilities well or badly depending on the incentives SBA presents them.

The theme of this chapter is the efficiency and cost-effectiveness of current program incentives. The primary question is whether by restructuring its relationship with banks, SBA could achieve the same level of performance, or percentage of successful loans, at lower cost. The answer is yes, by reducing the guarantee percentage to between 65 percent and 80 percent.

This chapter first briefly describes the cost of the program to SBA, the program subsidy. It then turns to the efficiency of the agency relationship with banks and the effect of the guarantee percentage.

LEVEL OF SUBSIDY

Though program supporters may not like to admit it, the SBA loan guarantee program is clearly subsidized. The federal government loses money on purchased loans, and spends money for program administration. The guarantee fees it collects offset only a small part of these costs. If we compare the present value banks receive on SBA loan portfolios (0.99 percent of original value) to the value the portfolio would have had without the guarantee (0.90 percent of original value, both figures from preceding chapter), it appears that the subsidy is about 9 percent of original principal. The estimate only includes the cost of loan losses less the guarantee fee. The author's calculations show that SBA loses about $0.58 of every $1.00 it spends to purchase loans.

The subsidy is the grant equivalent of the program. From SBA's financial perspective, the guarantee transaction is equivalent to giving each borrower 9 percent of the loan amount in cash. As average loan size varies from year to year in the range of $155,000 to $170,000, this amounts to between $14,000 and $15,000 per borrower.

SBA's own administrative expenses are an additional subsidy. SBA must pay for a review of each loan application by its district staff and for the collection of purchased loans. In addition, SBA maintains staff in its Washington headquarters, some of whom are devoted solely to the business loan program. A rough estimate of 1984 SBA administrative expenses for the loan guarantee program is $68.5 million.[1] This is slightly more than 2 percent of new loans guaranteed in 1984.

If this estimate of SBA administrative expenses is added to the subsidy paid on loan defaults, the total subsidy on a new loan is about 11 percent, or $321 million for the program as a whole in 1984. Comparable figures for 1986 are $88.5 million in administrative expenses, which was 2.9 percent of new loans. This is offset by the increase of the guarantee fee in 1986 from 1 to 2 percent. The total subsidy in 1986 was thus $286 million. In the same year the Office of Management and Budget, using a methodology that compared the cost of the SBA guarantee (that is, the guarantee fee) to the premium private insurers would require in order to insure the same portfolio, estimated the subsidy to be 12.2 percent of loan volume.[2]

While the subsidy is equivalent from SBA's financial perspective to giving each borrower a modest grant, it is quite different programmatically. It is ironic that the tangible subsidy in a loan guarantee program always goes to the failures. Successful borrowers repay all funds with interest, while failures receive large effective grants in the form of loan principal they do not repay. One might question whether a grant to each would be more equitable or effective than a bailout to some. In this instance, however, a grant program would not likely be an effective substitute. It is always hard to ensure that financial assistance for business is used to increase business activity, and with grants it is particularly so. The repayment requirements of loans tend to tie them to revenue generating activities. Lacking in such a connection, grants can easily serve merely to increase profits. Moreover, the real purpose of the SBA guarantee is to enable more businesses to obtain credit. Such borrowers may need and want a $160,000 loan more than a $15,000 grant. A loan guarantee may be the most cost-effective way of getting credit to such businesses, despite the ironies it creates. The question remains as to whether the government could get loans to its successful borrowers for a smaller subsidy.

The subsidy is also the federal expenditure equivalent of the SBA program, and therefore, it is now appropriate to mention an SBA budgeting issue briefly. The subsidy is the closest equivalent for a loan guarantee program to the direct expenditure concept on which budgeting for most federal activities is based. According to most students of federal budgeting principles, it should be recorded in the budget together with SBA administrative expenses in the year each cohort of loans is guaranteed, and used as the basis for appropriations of budget authority for the program.[3] Instead, only 1.5 percent of loan volume and SBA's administrative expenses are appropriated in the year of guarantee. The costs which remain, the majority of the total, are appropriated in the year in which defaults occur. The Congress has no discretion over these payments; they occur after the point of commitment, and hence decision making, has passed. Principles of good budgetary accountability require that the impact of future obligations be assessed at the point of governmental discretion. As it stands, the delay gives the loan guarantee program a budgetary advantage over direct expenditures which are fully appropriated in the first year. If a budgeting rule were adopted that placed SBA on an equal footing with other uses of federal resources (that is, 9 percent of new loans guaranteed are appropriated in their initial year) SBA would face a greater incentive to improve efficiency and accomplish the same purposes at lower budget cost.

HOW BANK INCENTIVES AFFECT SBA RETURNS

Banks are the key to the success or failure of the loan guarantee program, both financially and a means of achieving public goals. As is so often the case for the federal government, the government in this program has few direct links with its intended beneficiaries, the small businesses. Instead, it employs thousands of agents, mainly commercial banks, to act on its behalf. Everything from the level of subsidy to the type of businesses assisted is determined by banks acting under SBA's guidance.

But bank behavior is not a wild card. Banks act predictably in accord with their own profit-making and customer development objectives. By understanding those objectives, and the effect of its program on them, SBA can predict how banks will respond.

SBA's relationship to banks is one of the wide class known as principal-agent relationships, the classic example being that of a client and stockbroker. Such relationships arise when a principal gives an agent the authority to make decisions that will have a direct effect on some objective valued by the principal, such as the value of his stock portfolio. The authority is delegated because the agent possesses comparative advantages in making the required decisions. Agency relationships work well when the principal pays the agent according to a fee schedule that varies with the success of the choices. The amount the agent actually receives should depend both on the agent's capabilities and on his response to the incentives presented in the fee schedule. Incentives should be structured so that the more the principal makes the more the agent receives, within the limit that an efficient agency relationship is one in which the principal's objectives are furthered for the lowest possible fee. If an agency relationship is inefficiently structured, it should be possible to improve the agent's performance without increasing the principal's cost.

The choice of banks as agents offers the government many definite advantages. Banks are expert in business lending and have administrative structures that should enable them to evaluate borrowers more accurately and administer loans more cheaply than SBA can. In addition, banks have a profit motive that pushes them toward efficient performance. SBA, as a government entity supported by the budget, cannot share this motivation, no matter what the quality of its civil servants may be. Geographic dispersion is another advantage. Banks have offices in every town and locality, while SBA is limited to more important centers. This enables banks to observe borrowers more closely and to be more familiar with local economies. Their network of financial services also provides banks with greater leverage over borrowers than SBA would have. Such services, the simplest and perhaps most powerful being checking accounts, bind borrowers to banks, and make them more likely to fulfill repayment obligations. Finally, SBA delegates to banks because it hopes to foster ongoing linkages between banks and target businesses, and to alter the way banks approach small business lending in general.

That SBA recognizes the magnitude of these advantages is evidenced by the fact that the direct loan program has been allowed to atrophy, in favor of guarantees. Within the guarantee program, SBA's heavy reliance on banks is evidenced by SBA's low rejection rates of completed guarantee applications its offices receive from banks. While SBA does turn back many applications, the rejections are usually due to incomplete documentation. A high proportion of these are resubmitted and approved. An SBA official in charge of lender relations stated that SBA approved 90 percent of all completed applications banks submitted. Bankers corroborated this figure in interviews. SBA may have a somewhat greater role in modifying proposed loan terms, but by and large, even though a great deal of SBA staff time is used in reviewing applications, SBA relies heavily on the judgment of banks to choose borrowers. Moreover, it relies completely on banks to manage and service the loans that have not yet defaulted.

The fee schedule SBA sets forth for its agents is not a schedule per se. Rather, SBA creates a schedule in effect through the rules it sets out for banks. The main elements are the guarantee, the fact that the guarantee is partial, the guarantee fee banks pay SBA, regulations on how much banks can charge (interest rate ceiling, prohibition against fees and compensating balances), borrower eligibility rules, and finally, administrative requirements. An important aspect of this fee structure is that its value is not evident on its face. The elements take on values in combination with the bank's own operating methods and expenses, as discussed in the previous chapter. The actual fee schedule cannot be known until it is shown how the costs and returns banks normally face as well as the lending opportunities they find among prospective borrowers interact with the rules of the SBA program. Thus, while SBA knows clearly what incentives and regulations it has set out, it does not know the value of those incentives unless it can translate them into costs and returns for banks.

The model of the financial impact of the program on banks, detailed in the previous chapter, accomplishes that translation, and also indicates which point on the schedule the lenders choose. The present values actually experienced reflect the agents' responses to the incentives the fee schedule contains. Knowledge of this provides the clues necessary to make hypotheses about the effect of changes in the fee schedule that could be enacted to improve the program.

SBA receives its payoff or outcome as principal in the form of the loan portfolio the program generates. The value of this outcome is defined ultimately by the program's social and economic goals. These goals are the main subjects of the next chapter. At this stage we only refer to two intermediate objectives that are integral to the program's function, no matter what its final aims are. The first of these is to accomplish program tasks at the least possible cost, and the second is to maximize the number of successful loans attributable to the program. In other words, these intermediate objectives amount to considering whether SBA has structured its agency relationship efficiently. The remainder of this section uses information on returns to banks and bank behavior to evaluate the efficiency of each element in the fee structure.

The Effect of the Guarantee

The starting point, and by far the most important element, is the guarantee. The major function of this or any loan guarantee is to induce banks to change their lending patterns toward borrowers they would not otherwise serve or would serve only on stricter terms. The guarantee accomplishes this by drastically reducing the effect of default on bank returns. The guarantee is intended to guide bank selection of borrowers. From SBA's point of view, banks can make the wrong selection in either of two ways. If banks lend to those who would otherwise have received credit, they are committing one type of selection error; if the program merely mimics private decisions, SBA has accomplished nothing of its own. On the other hand, it is not desirable for banks to be indiscriminate in choosing borrowers. If banks lend to borrowers who are too likely to default or manage loans in ways that increase the chances of default they will have created another type of error. To avoid this error, the guarantee is left only partial. Banks are given some incentive to choose loans "reasonably to assure repayment," as the Small Business Act requires.

It is a problem in the design of any loan guarantee program that the aims of changing bank lending patterns and minimizing defaults conflict. For SBA, the conflict arises first because banks tend to have selected the most credit worthy clients already, so that any change necessarily brings a higher default portfolio. More importantly, the guarantee invites banks to disregard default risk. As this conflict is inevitable in any risk-sharing arrangement, the partial guarantee level should be set so as to achieve the best balance between the two aims. The available evidence suggests that the SBA program allows a large number of both types of selection errors to occur. With regard to the first type, it is quite difficult to tell how many borrowers would have received substantially the same type of credit in the absence of the guarantee. The guarantee clearly convinces banks to make different loans from their normal ones in most cases. This is evidenced by the long maturities of SBA loans and the high proportion of new and minority businesses that receive them as well as by the high default rate.

The model of bank returns suggests that banks would have little reason to apply an SBA guarantee to a loan it would already make, unless it were a borderline case. Consider a group of private loans whose probability of default is average for private bank loans, that is only one tenth as high as that for SBA loans. Its present value is just above 1.01, the average private level (as in Table 3.2). If a bank were to apply an SBA guarantee to such a group of loans (at the same interest rate) their probability of default would stay the same but their value in the event of default would rise from 16 percent to 75 percent of the amount outstanding at the time of default. Costs of administration would go up 10 percent because of SBA paperwork and the bank would have to pay SBA a one percent guarantee fee. The present value of this group of loans with guarantee is calculated to be just below 1.01, slightly below the value without the guarantee. The extra protection afforded by the guarantee would be absorbed by the added cost and guarantee fee, and there would be no advantage to joining the loans to the SBA program. Banks could pass this fee to borrowers, but faced with higher costs, high quality borrowers would look elsewhere for credit. If, without the guarantee, the bank would normally have charged its own origination fee or required a compensating balance, both prohibited under SBA, there would be a greater disadvantage.

For loans with above average default probability, but still within the range banks allow, there could be a positive gain in present value. The extent to which guarantees are applied to loans at the riskier end of current bank practice remains an open question.

Yet bankers report that a significant portion (about 20 percent) of their clients would have been eligible for credit without the guarantee. The answer probably lies in the fact that SBA loans are often used to give already credit worthy borrowers larger loans and loans of longer maturity than they would otherwise qualify for. Thus, for many of SBA's loans, a portion of the total loan amount substitutes for private lending and a portion is incremental.

The error of mimicking private activity is a neutral error. From SBA's perspective, the guarantee costs nothing and has achieved nothing. The second type of error, high defaults, is of greater concern because it is expensive to SBA. The guarantee protects banks almost completely from bearing the consequences of poor decisions. As we saw above, banks' returns are not very sensitive to defaults once the guarantee has been applied. The maximum gain in returns from completely eliminating default is only 1.5 to 1.9 percent. Within more realistic ranges of decreasing defaults, the gains are much smaller.

The costs to SBA, by contrast, vary significantly, even over small variations in default probability. In fact, there is a wide range of default probabilities across which banks are likely to be practically indifferent while SBA is not. To illustrate, consider the financial effect on SBA of various bank strategies to improve returns, which were shown in Table 3.3. The strategies of lowering default rates and particularly of increasing collateral coverage are relatively unattractive to banks, while they produce great improvement for SBA. Most striking is the result that if a bank increased the default rate by neglecting administrative duties it could probably still increase its returns, while causing the SBA a significant loss.[4] It is also interesting to note that SBA's costs are virtually invariant to bank decisions on interest rates, which could make a significant difference to banks.

In summary, SBA has set up a fee schedule for banks that gives banks little incentive to minimize SBA's cost. This indicates that the principal-agent relationship is not efficient. The observation that bank returns are relatively invariant with respect to SBA's strongly implies that the guarantee percentage should be reduced.

Variation in Guarantee Percentage. Most people seem to view the default rate in the SBA program as the inevitable consequence of lending to the types of borrowers SBA wishes to serve. Congressional hearings on SBA are full of remarks to the effect that the program must have a high default rate in order to reach its intended beneficiaries, or even more extreme, that high defaults are evidence that SBA is doing its job and is needed. This view would hold simply that SBA borrowers are ten times more likely to default than average private borrowers. Banks often put this argument forward to emphasize the need for at least a 90 percent guarantee to make their participation possible. Congress has responded to such arguments by passing legislation setting 90 percent as the minimum guarantee level for loans of less than $100,000, or since 1986, $155,000. Part of this reasoning is correct. The SBA program is likely to have higher defaults as long as it is aiming at a group not now served by banks. However, it is not appropriate to reason backwards. The observed default rate could result from causes other than inherent characteristics of the desired target group. Specifically, it could result in part from bank carelessness, as is likely given the lack of incentives banks face.

SBA cannot distinguish how much of the default rate it observes is a characteristic of the group it wishes to reach and how much a characteristic of bank laxity. Therefore, it must be sure that it has given banks incentives to select borrowers carefully. The most appropriate way to view the default rate is as the result of banks' responses to the level of protection offered by the guarantee. Because banks have such a wide range of discretion to choose and manage borrowers, they clearly have a sufficient range of choice to determine, within a reasonable range, the rate of default among borrowers.

In the comparison of the present values to banks of SBA loans and private loans (Table 3.2) it is striking that most costs, including default costs (postguarantee) are about the same. This suggests a fruitful line of speculation concerning the relationship between bank practices for regular and SBA loans. Bankers claim that they follow normal lending practices as far as possible when dealing with SBA loans. Normal lending practices for most banks include target levels of default and administrative costs for their private portfolios, which they and their examiners monitor closely. One very simple way for banks to follow "normal lending practices" for SBA loans, would be to apply these same targets to SBA loans, after the guarantee. Even if they do not follow this rule precisely, it is almost certain that banks making more than a few SBA loans would set limits on post-guarantee losses, and that these limits would not exceed their ordinary limits by much. What would happen if banks act this way? They would tolerate defaults on SBA loans to the point where the costs they bear reach the level of private loans. The direct conclusion would be: A reduction in the consequences of default to one tenth its ordinary level allows banks to make loans ten times as prone to default.

If this is an accurate description of bank decision making, it would be

Figure 4.1
Effect of Guarantee Percentage on Default Rate (default rate that equalizes present value)

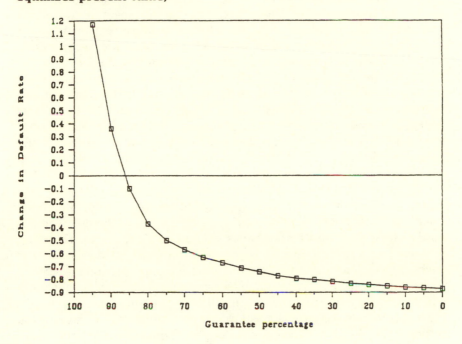

Guarantee percentage

possible for SBA to achieve whatever default rate it wishes by choosing the appropriate guarantee percentage. Banks would respond by setting the postguarantee default level of SBA loans to the target. Continuing reductions in the guarantee percentage would cause bank returns to fall eventually to the unguaranteed level, provided that the underlying default rates stayed the same. But the default rate would not stay the same. Faced with a lower guarantee, banks would equate postguarantee default costs with the target by selecting borrowers with lower default probabilities. The default rate thus becomes a function of the guarantee percentage.

This functional relationship is illustrated in Figure 4.1. In this figure, the assumption is made that banks want to limit postguarantee default costs to the level they currently receive for SBA loans. The figure shows the default rate that would result for the program at various guarantee percentages. As the guarantee percentage moves from 100 percent to 80 percent, banks must make large reductions in the default rate to produce the present values they currently receive. Below 65 percent the reductions in the default rate would be far slower.

If SBA and the Congress used this relationship to help select an appropriate guarantee percentage, they could achieve a significant reduction in the program's default rate by lowering the guarantee percentage from the 87 percent average it had for most of the 1980s to a level between 80 percent and 65 percent. As of 1986, SBA began using a range of 70 to 85 percent for its larger loans. The effect of this improvement on the default rate cannot yet be determined. The effect of a 75 percent guarantee is beginning to be evidenced in the low defaults associated with the preferred lender program, as discussed in Chapter 6. The predicted effect is that at 75 percent the default rate would be approximately halved. Below some level, probably 65 to 50 percent, banks would cease to have any interest in the program, as they would have to guarantee borrowers that would appear nearly as credit worthy as current ones. As the difference in port-folio quality at guarantee percentages between 80 and 65 percent is still substantial, showing that a different borrowing group would still be served, few banks would be likely to withdraw at these levels.

The success of a reduction in the guarantee percentage would depend on the bank's ability to target a higher quality borrower population than it has served without major increases in administrative expense. There is no direct evidence on whether banks would be able to do so. However, in a review of several small business loan programs in developed and developing nations, the American SBA loan guarantee program was found to have among the highest rates of guarantee coverage, showing that banks will participate in the programs even at lower guarantee rates.[5]

As the guarantee percentage is lowered the congruence between bank returns and SBA costs is increased. Closer congruence is the hallmark of an efficiently structured agency-principal agreement. It is clear that the current agreement is less efficient than one specifying a lower guarantee percentage.

Interest Rates

After the guarantee the most important influence SBA has over returns to banks is the regulation of charges. This includes both the interest rate ceiling and the prohibition against origination fees, compensating balances, and the like. The interest rate ceiling on SBA loans has concerned policy makers almost as much as has the guarantee percentage and has been the subject of many congressional hearings. The ceiling on the allowable rate stands at present and since 1979 at 2.25 percent above the published New York prime for loans of maturity less than seven years and 2.75 percent above prime for loans of seven or more years.

Although the present values of loans to banks are highly dependent on interest rates, they are not important in determining SBA's costs. If SBA's payoffs are indifferent to rates while banks' are not, it may seem odd that SBA constrains banks from charging more. The ceiling is usually justified as a matter of fairness to borrowers. Concern is often voiced by small business advocates that the ceiling is needed to insure that unscrupulous lenders do not charge SBA borrowers too much. As a result, the interest rate ceiling has generally kept SBA loan rates close to rates on similar private loans (Figure 3.2), and sometimes below private rates.

As seen above, loans are often made below the ceiling, demonstrating that competitive forces are frequently more restrictive than the regulation. This observation would indicate that the ceiling should be removed.

In another sense, however, the ceiling rate acts as a limit on the default rate. According to theory, the borrowers willing to pay higher rates would carry greater default risk than other SBA borrowers. In investigations of issues like credit rationing such a willingness is often believed to exist among risky borrowers. Normally the additional risks to lenders at these levels rise as fast or faster than the interest rate. If banks lent to such borrowers under the guarantee program, however, they would find that a slightly greater interest rate would completely cover their losses from a much greater default rate. The interest rate ceiling prevents them from doing this, and so, though intended to protect borrowers, it may protect SBA as well. If the guarantee percentage were lower, banks would have to raise interest rates higher to make up for the same increase in default probability, and this would make them self-restraining. As long as the guarantee remains at 90 percent, the interest rate ceiling may be serving as a protection against even higher defaults. The same principle applies to prohibitions against fees and compensating balances.

Whether or not SBA continues the interest rate ceiling, it is clear that it should switch from the prime rate to a long-term rate as the basis for the ceiling. During times when the yield curve is normal, long-term rates can sometimes be so much higher than short-term ones that banks, constrained according to a rate that varies with short-term rates, would avoid making SBA loans. Such a situation may have prevailed during 1982 when the average rate on SBA loans was just at the ceiling. The attractiveness of SBA loans to banks should not be a function of the yield curve.

Eligibility Rules

A final way in which SBA directs bank actions is by designing rules for eligibility of borrowers and of loan terms. SBA's costs are not affected by these choices, except to the extent that they cause default probabilities to change. However, as will be discussed in the next chapter, the benefits produced by the program are quite dependent on which firms receive credit and what kind of credit they receive. SBA's rules give banks wide discretion, so it is important to consider whether the choices they are likely to make fit SBA's goals.

NOTES

1. This estimate is developed from data in SBA's annual report for 1986, with the assumption that the finance and investment program expenses are 75 percent attributable to the loan guarantee program, and that nonprogram administration costs can be distributed proportionally among the various SBA programs.

2. U.S. Office of Management and Budget, *Budget of the United States Government, FY 1988*, Special Analysis F, "Federal Credit Programs," p. F–37.

3. See, for example, Alice M. Rivlin and Robert W. Hartman, "Control of Federal Credit" in Albert T. Sommers, ed., *Reconstructing the Federal Budget: A Trillion Dollar Quandary* (New York: Praeger, 1984), and Congressional Budget Office, "New Approaches to the Budgetary Treatment of Federal Credit Assistance," 1984.

4. The example in the table is illustrative only, because there is no way to estimate the effect of halving maintenance costs on default probabilities. However, the small variation in bank costs relative to high variation in SBA's is undisputed.

5. Deloitte Haskins and Sells, "Report on Loan Guarantee Mechanisms and other Financial Sector Innovations in Kenya," Unpublished, Nairobi, Kenya, 1985.

5 The Loan Guarantee Program from a Social Welfare Perspective

In the previous chapter judgments were made on the SBA loan guarantee program purely from an efficiency point of view: Does the program carry out its appointed functions without undue cost? This is a kind of minimum competency standard that should be set for any public program.

It is now time to turn to the more fundamental—and controversial—question: Does the program achieve its real social and economic goals? Does it fulfill its important public purposes? As described below, there is a general consensus on what those goals are. Creation and continuation of the SBA program is justified through references to them, and skepticism that it achieves these goals is at the root of the Reagan administration's repeated attempts to quash the program. Despite the repeated onslaught, program supporters have made little effort to evaluate how well SBA does. The model of the behavior and interactions of borrowers, banks, and SBA developed in the previous chapters, as well as some of the specific numerical findings, can help give some indication of whether the SBA program meets its fundamental public objectives.

This long but important chapter is organized as follows. First, there is a brief description of the social and economic goals commonly claimed for the program. These can be loosely classified into two main types for purposes of evaluation: correction of flaws in credit markets and contribution of social and economic benefits (externalities) by assisted firms. A third rationale, assisting disadvantaged groups, is relevant to a small portion of the program. The next section of the chapter examines the market imperfection rationales more closely, first explaining how markets are presumed to be flawed, then assessing whether the program corrects for the flaws. The remainder of the chapter examines the externality rationales. Again, the rationales are first described in more detail, then program achievement is assessed.

PROGRAM GOALS

Although there is grave disagreement as to whether the loan guarantee program is successful at achieving its goals, there is widespread acknowledgement of what those goals are supposed to be.

The first chapter pointed out that the creation of the SBA program was predicated on beliefs about the nature of business credit markets, centering on the opinion that commercial banks would not or could not provide credit (especially medium- and long-term) to small businesses. The original decision makers also described small businesses as necessary for the preservation of competition in the economy. The program was created to fill the credit market gap and help preserve the role of small businesses.

These reasons for the program have persisted and the list has grown. In one of the few articles published on the program, Richard Klein has assembled a list of the objectives cited most often. His is a convenient summary of statements that can be found throughout public testimony. It includes the following: promoting competition; overcoming small business credit gaps; allowing small banks to participate in a larger risk pool, thereby expanding their lending to small business; aiding socially or economically disadvantaged business owners; and promoting technological innovation and job creation.[1] An additional objective not included in Klein's list but mentioned often is the protection of small business from the effects of business cycles. The list is long, which is in itself a problem signal; no program can focus well on such diverse, and often implicitly contradictory, aims.

In order to come to grips with this list of goals, we divide them into groups, in accordance with standard categories used in the field of political economy to justify government intervention in the economy. This allows the principles of political economy to be applied to the SBA program in searching for a justification for it. There are three such explanations relevant to the SBA program: first, an imperfection in business credit markets; second, the generation of external benefits by beneficiaries; and third, distributional motivations to aid a particularly deserving group. The income distribution goal will be treated along with the externality goal, though important differences between them will be highlighted. Externalities are a type of market imperfection, but for clarity the two terms will be used separately here. The term market perfecting will only apply to inefficiencies in the financial markets, while externalities will refer only to benefits associated with the loan recipients and their firms.

The individual goals stated above fit nicely into these three categories. Overcoming credit gaps, protection against business cycle swings, and increasing risk pooling are credit market perfection objectives. Promoting competition, technological innovation, and job creation are external benefit objectives, and aiding socially or economically disadvantaged business owners is a distributional aim.

It is not surprising that public statements about goals can so easily be fit into the categories of welfare economics. Public debate on program goals usually stakes out a high moral ground by implicit reference to a concept of the general public good that is quite similar to that on which welfare economics is based. Desire to act for the general good is an important motivation for policy makers' decisions. It is important in what policy makers say about program goals, even when purely political motivations are paramount. In public debate a convention of interest in the public good is both a means to convince other participants in the political process and a matter of political decorum, which demands that bare self-interest be covered most of the time.

Furthermore, in most American public forums the market is regarded as the primary means of allocating economic goods. It is generally agreed that the government need not become involved in such allocation unless the results produced by the market are unsatisfactory. Three of the ways the market can produce an unsatisfactory result are the basis for the categories just listed. The political economist's categories for the SBA loan guarantee program—or almost any economically-oriented government program—can be viewed as more formal and thoroughly articulated versions of widely held, everyday rationales.

This chapter discusses each of these three social objectives, taking credit market imperfections first, and then combining the discussions of borrower externalities and distributional goals. The major findings are these. Because the program contains such a large subsidy for default, any claim that it corrects an error by credit markets is weak. Unless the program is restructured, this claim is not a valid basis for program justification. Distributional goals, in the form of lending to various minority or disadvantaged groups, are met to a degree by the program, but cannot be a major raison d'être, as 85 percent of all clients are not in one of these groups. With respect to externality goals, the information presented here cannot conclusively state whether the SBA borrowers produce enough benefits to compensate for the subsidy. It does show, however, that in order to compensate for program costs, each successful loan must result in additional benefits worth from 17 to 29 percent over and above the level of achievement needed to stay in business. While the ability of successful SBA loans to produce such benefits is unknown, one important point is clear: SBA makes little effort to insure that banks will target borrowers with especially high benefit potential. The conclusions on each major social goal suggest that a restructuring of the program is in order.

CORRECTING FLAWS IN SMALL BUSINESS CREDIT MARKETS

When the SBA program began, commercial banks provided little term credit for small businesses, providing virtually all small business credit as 90-day overdrafts. This was perhaps the strongest reason for creating the new program. Several prominent studies had shown that bank service to small firms was inadequate, and it was believed that banks might never be able to provide term credit profitably. In discussing the origins of the SBA a GAO study stated,

In the 1930's, 40's and early 50's the Department of Commerce, the Federal Reserve Board, and others conducted independent studies of small business financing. These studies concluded that a serious credit gap existed for small and medium size businesses because their access to equity and bond markets was limited and banks were generally reluctant to lend them money on a long-term basis.[2]

Commercial banking has evolved since that time, and term loans are regularly made to firms of the sizes SBA handles, particularly in the intermediate term range. This has reduced the scope and power of the credit market flaw argument, but has not fundamentally altered it.

The basic premise of current arguments is that small firms are offered proportionally less credit or credit on poorer terms than larger firms *of equal credit risk*. According to the argument, this results from problems inherent in the functioning of financial institutions and credit markets, not from a failing on the part of the smaller borrowers. Many of these claims are accurate.

Small firms have fewer options for securing finance, particularly long-term finance, than large firms. They do not have access to the bond market, which is the major source of long-term debt for large businesses. They cannot enter bond or equity markets because the costs of underwriting are too high relative to the amount of funds they require. Underwriting has a high fixed component; the costs of gathering and then distributing information on a small firm differs little from that on a large one. As the volume of funds raised in a single bond issue increases, the proportional cost of underwriting falls. In a survey covering the early 1970s the Securities and Exchange Commission found that for equity issues up to $500,000 (the maximum SBA loan size) the administrative cost of issuance was 24 percent of the total funds raised, while for issues over $20 million it was as low as 5 percent.[3] Bond issues exhibit a similar pattern. Among the size range of businesses SBA serves, these costs are prohibitive. In fact, SBA has used size at which entry into equity and bond markets becomes infeasible as a working definition of small business in deliberations over SBA eligibility rules.[4]

Without access to bond or equity markets, small businesses must rely on commercial banks as their primary sources of funds. But while businesses often require long-term credit, commercial banks prefer to supply only short-term loans. In interviews bankers reported three or sometimes five years as the longest terms bank policies allow, except for commercial mortgages, which are available for long terms because of the lifespan of the collateral. Federal Reserve data on the composition of business debt outstanding at commercial banks shows that about half has maturities of less than one year. The average maturity on the remaining half was 3.5 years (for the years 1977 to 1983). The preference for short-term lending derives primarily from the asset and liability structure of commercial banks. Banks must maintain liquidity by avoiding a mismatch between the maturities of their mostly short-term liabilities and their assets. This short-term liability structure may be accentuated by the increasing use of certificates of deposit rather than savings accounts. Banks also attempt to avoid interest rate risk, which can be quite large on long-term, fixed rate loans.

The short-term preference may also result from the short life of the collateral businesses have to offer. Banks reduce their risk of loss by obtaining liens on specific tangible assets. The collateral on commercial and industrial term lending, often the assets purchased with loan funds, has market value for only a few years. In the matter of valuing collateral there may be a fundamental difference in perspective between borrower and lender because the market life of assets is shorter than their useful lives in the original business. Businesses wish to obtain financing whose repayment parallels the stream of services they receive from an investment. Banks, on the other hand, wish to insure that the value of the assets in a liquidation sale will always equal or exceed the loan principal outstanding at the time of default. In theory, this problem would affect both large and small businesses, but large firms have alternate sources of long-term financing through the bond and stock markets.

The SBA loan guarantee program is said to overcome this "credit gap" by enabling banks to make longer term and larger loans to small customers. A GAO survey of commercial banks participating in the SBA program found that only 15 percent of all non-SBA small business loans have maturities over five years, compared to 74 percent of SBA loans. Since the survey also reports that 13 percent of small business loans among banks sampled are SBA-guaranteed, this would mean that 42 percent of all business loans over five years in maturity by participating banks are SBA loans. When asked to name why they participate in the SBA program, extension of longer maturity loans is one of the reasons bankers cite most frequently.[5] With regard to loan size, it is clear that SBA loans are much larger than private commercial loans, which average well below $100,000. It is generally believed that SBA loans are somewhat less highly collateralized than private loans, indicating that borrowers receive larger loans than they otherwise could. As seen earlier, the program certainly provides incentives for banks to lend larger amounts from a given collateral base.

Another quite different problem in credit markets is also said to affect small business, vulnerability to business cycles. Commercial banks are thought to refuse loans to small businesses during periods of tight credit and to raise interest rates disproportionately. They do so in order to continue to meet the demands of their large customers. There is considerable controversy over whether cyclical credit rationing occurs, but it might, for example, if higher loan administration costs of small business loans cannot be fully passed on as higher interest rates. According to some evidence on the income generated by various types of loans, small business loans offer a smaller return, due to higher costs not fully passed on, than do large ones. The small loan customers on the margin of profitability are therefore the first to be discarded. Moreover, large businesses command larger portions of valuable bank deposits, giving them better bargaining positions in tight credit times than small businesses have.

While such a cyclical effect may hurt small business borrowers, there is little evidence that the SBA program works to overcome it. SBA loan approval procedures have neither built-in countercyclical effects nor administered responses to cyclical conditions. If the program were countercyclical there would be an increase in the volume of new lending when credit is tight. Instead, lending levels are set in annual legislation, according to political rather than economic considerations. The program operates at or near its limit during most periods except severe downturns. Although more banks may favor SBA loans when they reach their liquidity limits, this cannot influence the total volume of loans SBA guarantees as long as the program is constrained by its limitation. Neither do the interest rates charged on SBA loans offer any relief, compared with rates charged on private loans.

An extreme example of the lack of response of both automatic features and policy occurred in 1982 when extremely high interest rates and severe recession coincided. The volume of SBA lending fell by 43 percent because rates offered on SBA loans were as high as available private rates, and no businesses wished to borrow long term. SBA administrators were in the midst of implementing a policy of higher standards of credit worthiness, and accordingly, they exerted further pressure in the same direction as the business cycle, not against it.

It is also plausible that the SBA program could counteract business cycles by protecting existing guaranteed loan borrowers against defaults brought on by unfavorable economic conditions. As shown in Chapter 2, holders of SBA loans remain quite vulnerable to business cycle conditions, though there is no basis to judge how vulnerable they would have been without the loans.

If the countercyclical argument is put aside, the main market-perfecting rationale for the SBA program recognizes the limitations of commercial banks as suppliers of long-term credit, and centers on SBA's ability to induce banks to lend at longer maturities and for larger amounts, thus affording small firms the same access to credit as similarly credit worthy large firms. If it were demonstrated that such flaws exist and that the SBA program is effective at solving them, this line of justification would win approval for the program from the widest possible political spectrum. Conservative and liberal alike approve of rectifying market imperfections.

Subsidies and the Market-Perfecting Aim

It is crucial to the credit market gap explanations of the program's purpose that small businesses be disadvantaged in credit markets not through any fault of their own, but simply because of the inability of financial institutions to cope with their size or their maturity needs. This statement points toward a high performance standard for judging whether the SBA program has corrected the credit market flaw. The argument locates the failing in the financial system or the size of the firm, and not in the credit worthiness of borrowers. The performance criteria are therefore those that would be applied if the financial system were operating without flaw. Specifically, the assisted small business borrowers should prove equally credit worthy as privately served borrowers. In other words, the portfolio should require no subsidy for default losses.

Many of those who make credit gap arguments in favor of the SBA program will not recognize that the argument implies such a high standard. Yet the standard is an unavoidable corollary of the argument, and it is important to recognize this in evaluating the usefulness of the loan guarantee program. Discrimination on the basis of credit risk is one of the functions credit markets are intended to perform. If banks are right that SBA's target group is too risky, the argument ceases to be one of perfecting credit markets, and is immediately converted into one of assisting risky businesses because of some deserving quality.

To illustrate, consider the effect of SBA loans to lengthen loan maturities beyond those banks normally provide. The source of bank reluctance to provide long-term loans could be the short-term deposit base most banks have, a result of institutional structure, and hence a credit market flaw. If, on the other hand, banks perceive longer term loans as too risky, and this turns out to be true, then the flaw is with the borrower. If credit markets appear to be operating efficiently, we would have to seek the rationale for the SBA program with the borrowers themselves, as is done in the next part of this chapter.

The credit market correction argument makes no reference to the borrowers or the uses of loans. Financial markets have no responsibility to allocate loans to businesses on the basis of social or economic criteria, but merely on financial ones. This is in direct contrast to the standard for evaluating the externality rationale. This might not be an important point were it not for the fact that SBA's eligibility guidelines are consistent with the market flaw standard in their lack of specific guidelines, as will be discussed below.

It should be clear that the high level of defaults among SBA guaranteed loans is far in excess of the market correction standard. Defaults require a 9 percent subsidy from SBA, or 11 percent, if SBA's administrative expenses are included. This fact discredits any claim that SBA loans correct a credit market failing. While the program does overcome gaps in the credit market, by changing the lending patterns of banks, it does so only by means of a subsidy. If the subsidy is to be justified, borrowers must be shown to produce some benefit that compensates for the subsidy's cost.

It is no surprise that SBA borrowers require a subsidy to cover default risk. This has been a characteristic of government business loan programs since RFC began the first one (although early subsidies were lower, according to available evidence). Government business loan programs have historically combined correcting markets and favoring borrowers thought to be particularly worthy. However, earlier programs, operating in simpler credit markets, could claim that a subsidy was required to achieve a demonstration effect. If a demonstration effect were present, some subsidy was acceptable in a market perfecting program. Such an effect was spectacularly shown when the Federal Housing Administration helped demonstrate that thirty year home mortgages could be profitable. For RFC, the demonstration effect is borne out by the fact that banks eventually learned to serve small business borrowers and to make longer maturity self-amortizing loans. In SBA's case, however, no such demonstration appears to be occurring. At present, SBA loans occupy the fringe of bank abilities in terms of loan maturities and loans to new borrowers and there is no indication that banks are moving in those directions on their own. Bank lending policies in this area have been fairly stable for two or more decades.

The demonstration effect argument is often used to defend loan guarantees to small business in developing countries. Dennis Anderson and Farida Khambata state that loan guarantees should introduce financial institutions to a target population previously excluded from private credit. This will enable lenders to learn to distinguish good credit risks within the group from bad. Eventually the lenders will learn to serve this population with no risk protection.[6] In SBA today, there may be some learning by banks regarding individual borrowers, but not about a general group of firms, as seen by the fact that bank lending practices have not altered recently.

The subsidies in the SBA program do not disprove that credit markets are flawed; they merely disprove that SBA corrects a flaw. As discussed in the previous chapter, banks have little incentive under the guarantee to select borrowers carefully and minimize the default rate. As long as these slack incentives remain, the level of defaults will continue to reveal more about the needs of banks than about the existence of a potentially successful group of borrowers. If SBA wishes to learn whether its program has the potential to find credit worthy borrowers who are discriminated against in financial markets, it will first have to improve bank incentives.

If one stops a moment to reflect on the structure of the loan guarantee program, the realization comes that the program is not really designed to address credit market failures. In the first place, the guarantee mechanism is not directed against structural problems, such as term deposits or high administrative costs. It is directed against credit risk, a borrower attribute. A program designed to address these other problems might offer a subsidy for administrative expenses on small loans, or a source of long-term deposits for long-term loans made to small businesses. In many countries small business credit programs are linked to discounting facilities that assure banks of long-term funds when they are needed. Moreover, the arguments that small businesses are disadvantaged in credit markets apply to all small businesses, whereas the SBA program assists only a small fraction. A program aimed more directly at correcting credit markets would affect a larger percentage of the small business population.

EXTERNAL BENEFITS BORROWERS PRODUCE

In the search for accomplishments attributable to the SBA program, arguments that SBA's borrowers produce social and economic benefits are of prime importance, particularly if the subsidy is to be justified. It is plausible to think that small businesses could generate extra benefits that could rightly be classified as externalities. One has only to observe the difference in perspective between lenders and public policy. Lenders are concerned with only a limited number of the outputs their borrowers produce. They care mainly that businesses produce the minimum amount of funds to maintain debt service and secondarily that they remain viable customers in the future. Equity holders go beyond this. They also value the firm's potential to produce extraordinary returns above the minimum required for debt service. A public policy or social perspective goes still farther. All the contributions a firm makes to the economic or social environment are valued, including those not captured by holders of a firm's debt or equity. When the credit decision includes only returns to lenders, even if credit markets judge costs and returns accurately, firms that are financially risky but offer high equity or social benefits will receive too little credit with respect to the total social and economic benefits they produce.

There are a number of benefits attributed at various times to small businesses. The externality claims center on three possible areas in which small businesses are said to excel: growth (especially employment growth), innovation, and competition. The SBA itself has stressed growth in its research and publications, stemming from initial work by David Birch, which, though its results have since been called into question, has been very influential in shaping opinions. His study is quoted by SBA as showing that 82 percent of new jobs were generated by small firms (less than 100 employees) during the 1970s.[7] According to SBA officials, job creation is a general concern of the loan guarantee program.[8] The rapid growth of high technology firms is the usual frame of reference for the claim regarding innovation. SBA states that, "The small firm contribution to innovation is widespread in such areas as instrumentation, consumer goods, and medical devices."[9] An older, but still valued idea is that small firms help create competitive conditions in capital markets, and are an antidote to monopoly power.

Distributional Motivations

A final goal named for the program is that of promoting business own-ership and growth among particularly deserving borrowers. The distinction between economic externality and income distribution goals is often blurred in public statements. The distinction should be kept clear, however. While the externality goal rests on an economically measurable (or potentially measurable) output by borrowing firms, the distribution goal rests on a desire to assist the firm owners themselves. The value ascribed to assisting people in the deserving groups is ultimately a political judgment.

There are three main groups mentioned in connection with the SBA program, economically disadvantaged business owners, members of racial or ethnic minorities and women. A tiny subset of the program serves handicapped business owners. It would be hard to classify owners of the firms SBA loans assist as economically disadvantaged. SBA loans do not reach the smallest firms. This is indicated in part by the fact that the average SBA loan size is significantly larger than the average private commercial and industrial loan. A critique of the SBA program from organizations working with the smallest enterprises is SBA's lack of responsiveness to their clientele. Although there are no statistics available on the financial standing of SBA-assisted business owners, few owners of firms eligible to borrow $155,000 (roughly the average) are likely to be in a low income group. To be eligible to borrow such a sum, the owners would have to have assets, both business and personal, worth a substantial portion of that amount, in the form of equity and collateral. SBA does have a smaller equal opportunity loan program targeted specifically on low income en-trepreneurs, but this is part of its direct loan program, which is outside the bounds of this study.

While some official SBA statements cite ownership of business by women as a goal, the proportion of SBA borrowers who are women is not different from the proportion of women-owned businesses in the economy. SBA makes no special effort to promote loans to women.

Only loans to minorities can really be considered a distributional purpose of the SBA program. In 1981 and 1982 about 10 percent of SBA loans (9 percent by dollar amount) went to businesses owned by members of ethnic or racial minorities. This is in contrast to minority ownership of about 5 percent of all firms. These figures are quite stable from year to year. Lending to minorities is clearly an objective of the program, but it is far from the program's main thrust.

Evaluating the Externality Rationale

A first cut at evaluating the accuracy of the external benefit claims can be made simply by reviewing SBA's borrower selection guidelines, loan policies, and actual lending patterns. SBA does not tell banks to assist especially fast-growing or innovative firms, or firms in industries with too little competition. It merely sets size and credit worthiness standards, and leaves the choice to banks. Without any such guidance, banks will not seek out such firms on their own initiative, except perhaps fast-growing ones. The result of the absence of a high-benefit strategy in borrower selection can be seen in the identity of the firms that receive SBA-guaranteed loans. To return to the words of program critic Stockman,

Unfortunately, neither stated SBA policies nor empirical analysis of SBA's lending patterns provide any evidence that subsidized SBA credit assistance serves *any focussed or rigorously defined public policy purpose at all*. In fact, the overwhelming bulk of SBA credit resources (60%) flow to a tiny fraction of non-credit worthy firms in mainstream *service, retail and wholesale sectors*.[10] (emphasis in original)

Stockman goes on to present data showing that 60 percent of all SBA loans go to locally oriented firms, termed "mainstreet merchants." By comparison, less than 3 percent of SBA loans went to the "sunrise industries," defined as high growth, high technology industries. Stockman also showed that the great majority of SBA loans go to firms in industries with low concentration ratios, and virtually none to highly concentrated manufacturing industries, "where large and small businesses actually compete."[11] Instead, he claims with some accuracy, SBA firms compete against other similar firms that do not have the benefit of federally assisted credit.

A comparison of SBA borrowers to all U.S. commerce and industry shows that the SBA pattern is essentially the same as the national one (Table 5.1). SBA is prohibited from lending to certain types of business activities, including real estate investment and finance. If this regulation

Table 5.1
Small Businesses Distributed by Industrial Sector (percent of all firms, by number)

Sector	All Small Businesses	All, Adjusted a/	SBA Borrowers
Wholesale	10	12	11
Retail	30	35	41
Services	22	26	20
Manufacturing	9	11	16
Finance	7	1	1
Transportation	4	5	3
Mining	1	1	1
Construction	14	6	6
Agriculture	3	3	3
Total	100%	100%	100%

Sources: Brookings Institution Small Business Data, and SBA.

a/ Finance and construction, areas where SBA is partially prohibited from lending, are constrained to same proportion
as for SBA.

is corrected for by constraining the proportion of such businesses to be the same proportion as SBA's activity in the sector, the adjusted distribution of SBA borrowers and all small businesses is virtually parallel. SBA lends to a slightly larger proportion of retail and manufacturing firms, and slightly fewer services. This probably results not from SBA policy, but from a higher frequency of term borrowing by manufacturers. SBA borrowers do tend to be firms serving local economies: stores, distributors, and restaurants.

In short, SBA firms are not distinguishable by type from all small business firms. Therefore, unless one accepts Stockman's conclusion that no public purpose is served, one must look deeper to find possible externality benefits. There are several possible ways that extra benefits could be produced.

• Banks may find it in their interest to select especially fast-growing firms.

• SBA loans themselves may have a growth-inducing impact, because they support capital investment.

• A high proportion of SBA loans (25 percent by dollar amount in 1978) go to new businesses,[12] while a much smaller proportion of businesses nationwide are new (4 percent in the same year).[13] Perhaps new businesses are particularly fast-growing and innovative.

• Finally, perhaps *all* small businesses produce the level of external benefits desired, so simply by serving ordinary small businesses, the SBA program succeeds.

In order to judge whether the program does in fact produce benefits in any of these ways, it is necessary to know more about the borrowers as individual businesses rather than aggregate categories, and particularly about the impact of SBA loans on them. For an assessment of the market-perfecting rationale, the program's financial performance was sufficient. For an assessment of its distributional impact it was necessary only to know how many borrowers fall into special groups. But for a judgment about the external benefits rationale, one needs to know what the businesses contribute to the economy, and how much of that contribution can be attributed to the SBA loan. This is exactly the type of information a standard program evaluation for such a program would seek.

Unfortunately, there are two obstacles to performing this type of evaluation. One obstacle is the lack of appropriate data and the other is the inherent limitation of an empirical approach in answering this question. Data requirements would include detailed information on individual borrowers covering several points in time. Items would include how loan funds were used, subsequent performance of the firm, and alternative sources of finance. Growth in value added or employment would be measured, and some estimate would be made of the extent to which these could be attributed to the receipt of the SBA loan. In contrast, SBA maintains only a few pieces of information about its borrowers, such as SIC code, size, age, and location.

To my knowledge, no study either within SBA or outside it has collected and analyzed the required type of information in a rigorous way. It may seem odd that given the long history of the program, the SBA would not have commissioned such a study. The reasons it has not are largely political and institutional. The first factor is that the SBA has focused on a model of the program that is basically credit market perfecting, resulting from its concern with banks. This leads the SBA's administration to pay relatively little attention to the impact of the loans on borrowers. Second, the research arm of SBA, which is responsible for commissioning studies, sees its mission as serving the whole of small business, and has therefore shown little interest in evaluating its own agency's programs. Third, private investigators have been deterred by SBA's protectiveness of the confidentiality of its borrowers. Perhaps a final reason is that the legislators considering program authorization have been content to rely on the anecdotal evidence supplied by loan recipients. In 1986 hearings before the House Small Business Committee, more than fifty individual business owners paraded to the stand to tell their success stories.

SBA ought to encourage a serious study, although it would be costly to carry out. A study with the purpose of examining what effect SBA loans have on their recipients could be an important contribution to an assessment of whether the program fulfills its aims.

Yet even if a detailed study of borrower behavior was available, its conclusions about the usefulness of the program would be limited. A second, less tractable obstacle would remain. If the aim of the program is to generate any of the benefits listed above, the central question is: How much more is produced than would have been produced without the program? The difficulty in answering it is that a dollar of federal aid will not generally yield a dollar of increased activity. How much more it produces depends on the elasticities of demand and supply for the parties involved, banks and borrowers. For SBA, as for other loan programs, the empirical problems of estimating elasticities are severe. Conclusions would be beset by problems of inference. There are many points at which an SBA dollar may go astray and not produce the intended outcome.

The most severe limitation concerns macroeconomics. At this level, an additional dollar of lending to one set of borrowers may be offset by reductions in lending to others. As discussed below, it is highly important to know how complete the offset is and which borrowers are squeezed out. Measurement of this effect would require the ability to discern how changes in the price and quantity of one type of financial asset result in changes in the price and quantity of other types, in the financial sector as a whole. Currently, the ability to measure such effects is quite limited.

At a microeconomic level, one needs to know what sources of finance borrowers would have used without SBA. The alternative to SBA assistance for many firms would have been some other form of perhaps more expensive financing, so that many of the loans cannot be said to increase the amount of credit available to recipients. Finally, it is difficult to estimate which of its many activities a recipient business would have omitted in the absence of a loan. The loan dollars are fungible. Asking borrowers themselves would not yield reliable answers. If they did not face the possibility of going without, they may never have formulated an alternative plan. Use of a control group is probably the best way to avoid this problem.

The task of combining all these escape routes into a defensible estimate of the increment to production attributable to the SBA program would be immense. Theoretically, the problems of information could be solved by the generation of increasingly complete data, and application of sophisticated statistical techniques. Limits, however, spring both from the cost of producing and analyzing the data and from questions of its reliability. Such practical limits to the application of sophisticated evaluation techniques are frequently encountered in assessments of economic incentive programs.

SBA must face the fact that it does not now and, except to a limited degree, possibly will not know the effect of its loan guarantee program on borrowers. The implications of that fact for program design for this, as well as for other programs, are serious.

When setting out to alter the behavior of an external entity—a firm, another governmental unit, or an individual—program designers must consider first how best to make the entity comply with the government's aim, and second, how to verify compliance. In the realm of regulation the importance of verification is recognized, because when coupled with penalties, verification helps increase compliance. Accordingly, to enforce pollution laws, great effort is devoted to designing efficient methods for monitoring. In nuclear arms control, the form of verification has strategic ramifications and is an essential part of negotiations.

Verification may sound like an odd term to apply to a program such as SBA's, where the aim is to induce an increase in certain economic activities such as job creation or innovation. However, the concept is quite comparable, and applies to a wide variety of programs, such as federal grants to state governments, student loans, and oil depletion allowances. Each of these programs uses incentives to encourage an entity outside the government to increase the volume of an activity it already performs to a lesser extent. Because incentives take the place of rules, verification seems a harsh word.

But the harshness is intentional. Fulfillment of the goal must be verifiable in order to tell whether the program is successful. If achievement of ultimate goals cannot be seen, a subtle change can take place in the actual operating objective of the program. The program tends to focus on outputs that are more readily observed. If the increment to production by SBA borrowers cannot be observed, the program can easily become transformed into an aid program for the recipient or the service provider, in this case the banks. This change can be seen in other programs besides the SBA. For example, the original goal of the student loan program was increased college enrollment. However, as it is difficult to assess what students would have done without the loans, the focus of policy turned to what could be observed, the number of students assisted. This has joined with distributional motives to transform the program into an aid program for college students. Its history shows a general movement from the first to the second goal, as eligibility restrictions have been eased.

In SBA's daily operations, simply providing a service to banks and small businesses has come to be regarded as the final objective for practical purposes, as evidenced by the traditional focus of SBA management information on number of loans approved. A general hypothesis for economic incentive programs might be that the extent to which the objective can remain focused in practice on the final outcome (incremental production) depends on the degree of verification possible.

Designers of a program facing an unobservable final outcome should consider seriously the possibility of reformulating its objectives to encompass only those outcomes which can be measured to at least some reasonable degree. Faced with such a dilemma, one sensible step would be to restructure goals so that they relate directly to the more observable criteria, rather than allowing a gulf to form between public goals and actual practice. For SBA, this would mean either a move toward a genuinely market-perfecting approach or toward targeting on clearly disadvantaged borrowers, as the chapter on reforms describes.

Minimum Benefit Level

Although we lack detailed information on the impact of SBA loans on borrowers, financial performance can shed some light on the externality rationale. The criterion for success of the SBA program in fulfilling the externality objective is that the value of such benefits attributable to the program (incremental benefits) must equal or exceed the subsidy; it must be at least 9 percent of loan value, or 11 percent with administrative costs. The idea that benefits must exceed the subsidy is simple and intuitive. While the loan performance that has been analyzed above does not show what form these benefits take, it permits measurement of the minimum size necessary to compensate for the subsidy and permits some inference about where the incremental benefits might originate. It is then possible to use aggregate information on SBA's borrowers to make an informed guess as to whether they are capable of producing the minimum required.

We can already state that not all SBA loans contribute to incremental benefits. Two groupings of loans logically cannot: loans that default and loans that would have been made on substantially the same terms without the guarantee. Behind most loans that default are firms that are failing or have failed, usually leaving the borrower in a worse financial position than before the loan. Defaulting firms are unlikely to produce unusually high levels of employment, productivity growth, or other social benefits. The social costs they incur may sometimes be even greater than the costs reflected in SBA default losses.

Loans that would have been made without SBA's help cannot be ascribed to the SBA program, nor can the returns the firms generate be said to originate from the program, even if they exceed the minimum level. This point not only applies to individual loans, it also applies to portions of loans, in cases where without the guarantee smaller or more expensive loans would have been forthcoming. We will call the loan dollars that meet these two tests successful incremental credits.

If all the external benefits SBA can claim must come only from successful incremental credits, the benefit burden per qualifying loan dollar is greater than 11 percent. Some rough calculations of the proportion of credits that qualify provide an estimate of how much greater it must be.

First, what proportion of all SBA loans are incremental, that is, would not have been made without SBA assistance? There is little hard information to go on in estimating this proportion, but general knowledge about the program suggests a few assumptions. The proportion of SBA lending to new and minority-owned firms is far greater than the proportion of private credit reaching them and than their relative share in the total small business population. A large share of the SBA loans to these groups would not have been made privately. To give SBA the benefit of the doubt, it is assumed here that all SBA loans to new and minority-owned firms are incremental. New firms receive 25 percent of SBA loans and minority-owned firms 9 percent (by dollar amount). Allowing for an expected 2 percent overlap between these two groups, we begin with a base of 32 percent of all SBA loans as incremental and therefore potentially externality-generating credits.

Remaining loans, 68 percent of the total, go to existing, nonminority firms. There are several reasons to believe that overlap with private credit among these loans is substantial. Some of the loans would have been made in essentially the same form without the guarantee. The last chapter pointed out that incentives are low for banks to attach a guarantee to loans for their average customers, but that incentives would be greater for borderline cases. Two recent surveys have asked commercial bankers what proportion of SBA-guaranteed loans they make to privately credit worthy borrowers on terms similar to those they would receive without the guarantee.[14] The responses indicated about 20 percent.

A second tier of borrowers would still have received loans, though with higher interest rates, shorter maturities, and smaller size. Bankers report that for a large portion of loans to existing, nonminority firms they use SBA loans for borrowers whose equity or collateral is insufficient to justify the amount of loan desired or for borrowers who seek an extended maturity loan. Thus, only a portion of each loan is additional to what would have been forthcoming privately. A complicating factor is that many SBA loans pay off the existing debts of the borrowers. A 1976 GAO study found that 11 percent of all loans in a sample paid off existing SBA loans, 19 percent refinanced existing loans to the guaranteed lender, and 22 percent paid off other creditors.[15] It is not known what portion of these figures overlap with each other. Nor is it known what proportion of the loan amount in each case was needed for the refinancing.

The available evidence on existing, nonminority firm loans are based on such different assumptions that they cannot be directly assembled into an estimate. They are sufficient to indicate that the incremental value of loans to such firms is significantly smaller than the total loan volume. Under these circumstances, it is best to offer a wide range of estimates. Accordingly, it is assumed that incremental credit among existing, nonminority firms falls between 25 percent and 75 percent of the total principal (Table 5.2).

This range would mean that between 17 percent and 51 percent of all SBA loans represent new or incremental credit for existing, nonminority firms. Combining these with loans to new and minority firms, a total of 49 percent to 83 percent of all SBA loan dollars can be assumed to be incremental.

Table 5.2
Social Benefit Required to Compensate for Subsidy (proportions of the value of all principal guaranteed)

	With high Duplication		With low Duplication a	
Successful incremental loans:				
Incremental loans (not-duplicated)				
To new firms	.25 x100%=	25.0%	x100%=	25.0%
To minority-owned firms	.09 x100%=	9.0%	x100%=	9.0%
Less overlap	.02 x100%=	-2.0%	x100%=	-2.0%
To existing, non-minority firms	.68 x 75%=	51.0%	x 25%=	17.0%
		------		------
Total incremental loans		83.0%		49.0%
Survival rate (loans not purchased)		76.5%		76.5%
		------		------
Total, successful incremental loans		63.5%		37.5%
Losses distributed across potentially beneficial loans:				
Subsidy as a percent of original principal		11.0%		11.0%
Distributed to successful incremental loans		17.3%		29.3%

a/ Duplication is guarantee of loans that private lenders would have made without the guarantee.

Among these incremental credits, a substantial percentage of borrowers default. The weighted average cumulative default rate found in Chapter 2 was 23.5 percent, or a survival rate of 76.5 percent (by number of loans). It is likely that the defaults occur more frequently among incremental loans (i.e., loans made to weaker borrowers or on more generous terms). However, for a conservative estimate, the overall 76.5 percent survival rate will be assumed. This leaves between 37.5 percent and 63.5 percent of total SBA loans as successful incremental loans. All the social externalities posited for the SBA program must come from this group of one- to two-thirds of all SBA borrowers. Note that the upper estimate of 63.5 percent is based on several generous assumptions. It is to be regarded as an upper bound. A best guess would be significantly lower.

If the subsidy is distributed evenly across all successful, incremental credits, the additional externality burden per loan is 17 percent to 29 percent of principal. This may be understood as the additional growth (or other benefit) that would be required by recipient firms over the life of the loan. It should be stressed that these benefits must be in excess of the minimum amount of growth required to enable a business to repay its loans. In essence, the successful loans must cross-subsidize the defaulting and duplicative loans. It must also be noted that the amount of growth must be additional to that which would be implied by loan repayment. If a company earns enough to repay its debts, it is also generating some amount of value added, employment and the like. As a class, SBA loans fall below that minimum. In order to avoid double counting, it is only the excess of value added, employment or other benefit, generated by successful loans, that can be counted against the losses generated by other borrowers.

The obvious next question is: Do SBA loans produce benefits of such magnitude? Here we reach the limits of the current analysis, and indeed, of SBA's own knowledge about its program. In the absence of a study on borrowers, conclusions about benefits must rest on information of a general nature about the types of firms SBA serves. As noted above, SBA firms are not distinguishable from other firms on the basis of industry. In fact, very few characteristics set them apart. SBA firms, in the aggregate, can be distinguished by small size, relatively weak financial condition (not credit worthy without the guarantee), and age (higher proportion of new firms).

The relative productivity of small versus large businesses is a matter of dispute. The supporters of the SBA believe small firms to be more productive and to generate greater social benefits than large firms, but this is not universally accepted. A great deal of complex evidence can be brought to bear on the question, which is beyond the scope of this study. It is important to remember, however, that the firms receiving SBA loans are not the smallest firms. They are more appropriately regarded as smallish to medium-sized firms.

One of the main characteristics that distinguishes SBA firms from other small businesses when they are selected is some weakness in financial position. All else being equal, a financially weak firm is less likely to grow rapidly or create new employment than a strong firm. This suggests that SBA firms would have more difficulty than the average in meeting the 17 to 29 percent requirement.

New businesses are hypothesized to grow faster than existing firms, and perhaps also to contribute to competition and innovation. However, nothing is known about the growth rates of the new firms receiving SBA loans. In summary, the knowledge of general characteristics of the borrowers helps little in ascertaining whether SBA firms produce more social and economic benefits than the average firms in the economy.

However, the possibility remains that SBA guaranteed loans are a catalyst to growth for the firms that receive them. SBA finances capital investment, which is crucial for start-up and major expansion. As term financing is somewhat scarce in the financial system, this is an important niche for SBA. By supporting major investment, SBA loans may help trigger especially productive periods. Similarly, SBA firms may be a foot in the bank door for many firms. If an SBA loan proves successful, a bank may be willing to make another loan to that borrower without a guarantee. The second loan could also be considered incremental, and benefits from it would add to the total ascribed to the initial loan.

In short, SBA firms are likely to be average performers in the economy, but SBA loans themselves may help the firms achieve more. The speculative nature of this conclusion only serves to emphasize how important it would be for SBA to carry out a systematic study of the business performance of its borrowers.

Even if it were known how SBA borrowers perform relative to all businesses, two doubts would remain, one relatively minor, and one crucial. The first question would be how well SBA borrowers would have to do to achieve the 17 to 29 percent added benefit level. Perhaps they would only have to equal all firms. If, as is quite possible, firms ordinarily make profits of at least that amount over the course of five to ten years, SBA borrowers would only need to do as well as the average.

The final question concerns the macroeconomic effect of the program on credit markets. If the total amount of credit in the system is fixed, as many believe, the program diverts a portion of that volume from market-selected uses to SBA-guaranteed loans. On the other hand, the program may add to the total volume of credit available. This macroeconomic question poses a very strong challenge not only against the SBA program, but against every attempt by the government to direct credit to uses it chooses. Unfortunately, techniques of macroeconomic estimation have not yet been able to answer the question of whether government credit programs change the total volume of credit, and certainly cannot answer it for a small, specific program like SBA guarantees. If the SBA program increases the volume, then it produces a positive net benefit as long as the firms meet the 17 to 29 percent target. If, however, it diverts credit from one group to another, SBA firms must meet a higher standard. They must reach the target simply to compensate for the subsidy, and they must provide an additional amount to compensate for the lost benefits that would have come from firms they have displaced. While it is plausible that SBA firms yield benefits as great as average firms, it is less likely that they are so much more productive than the norm.

To return for a moment to all three possible program goals, market perfection, external benefits, and income distribution, this chapter has concluded that the SBA program as now operated does not fulfill the first, and is not very well targeted at fulfilling the second or third. If the program is to be continued, it is clear that it should be restructured to pursue its goals more carefully, possibly choosing between them. The analysis of shortcomings just presented is useful for suggesting the directions reforms should take.

NOTES

1. Richard Klein, "SBA's Business Loan Programs," *Atlanta Economic Review* 28 (September-October, 1978): 28–37.

2. General Accounting Office, *SBA's 7(a) Loan Guarantee Program: An Assessment of its Role in the Financial Market*, GAO/RCED–83–96, April 1983, p. 1.

3. Quoted in Hans R. Stohl, "Small Firms' Access to Public Equity Financing" (Washington, D.C.: Interagency Task Force on Small Business Finance, December 1981).

4. Commission on Money and Credit, *Federal Credit Agencies* (Englewood Cliffs, N.J.: Prentice Hall, 1963), p. 436.

5. From interviews and General Accounting Office, *The Role of the SBA Loan Guarantee Program*, p. 91.

6. Dennis Anderson and Farida Khambata, "Financing Small-scale Industry and Agriculture in Developing Countries: The Merits and Limitations of 'Commercial' Policies," World Bank Staff Working Papers, No. 519 (Washington, D.C.: 1982).

7. Small Business Administration, *The State of Small Business: A Report of the President* (Washington, D.C.: March 1983), p. 85.

8. Interview with Charles Hertzberg, SBA Deputy Associate Administrator, October 1983.

9. Small Business Administration, *The State of Small Business*, p. 124.

10. David A. Stockman, quoted in U.S. Congress, House Committee on Small Business, *Financial Assistance Program Termination*, Hearings, 99th Cong., 2nd sess., 1986, p. 153.

11. Ibid., p. 167.

12. Small Business Administration, "7(a) Study as of September 30, 1978," internal document. There is no more recent SBA data available, but neither is there any indication that the proportions have changed significantly.

13. Candee Harris, with Nancy O,Conner and Kirk Kimmell, *Handbook of Small Business Data* (Washington, D.C.: The Brookings Institution, draft, January 1983).

14. General Accounting Office, *SBA's 7(a) Program*, p. 93. Cynthia Glassman and Peter L. Struck, "Survey of Commercial Bank Lending to Small Business" (Washington, D.C.: Interagency Task Force on Small Business Finance, January 1982), p. 88.

15. General Accounting Office, *The Small Business Administration Needs to Improve its 7(a) Loan Program*, February 1976, p. 98. Sample included direct loans, 12 percent of the total.

6 Special Programs

During the 1980s, the SBA developed three special programs within the main loan guarantee program that sought to address some of the problems that have been raised in the preceding chapters. These are the certified lender program, the preferred lender program, and the secondary market program. It is notable that the main intent or effect of all three has been to make the program more attractive to banks, without affecting borrowers directly. Each of the programs makes a contribution toward improving the efficiency of the agency relationship between banks and SBA, and each moves the loan guarantee program toward its market-perfecting aims. The greatest potential contribution comes from the preferred lender program. In fact, the preferred lender program is potentially so beneficial, that SBA should attempt to move as much of its portfolio into it as possible. The certified lender program has shown positive results, but it should be viewed primarily as a stepping stone to preferred lenders. The secondary market program provides a clear market-perfecting service, of significant positive value, within its limited objective.

CERTIFIED AND PREFERRED LENDER PROGRAMS

The certified and preferred lender programs are closely related efforts by SBA to restructure its relationship to banks. SBA describes the two programs as a shift from a retail to a wholesale approach in its delivery of services. The primary motivations behind the development of these innovations were to save SBA administrative costs and to make the program more attractive to banks. The method chosen was primarily greater delegation of authority to banks. This section discusses the effects of these innovations on program costs and benefits in light of the principal-agent relationship between SBA and banks.

In 1979 SBA initiated the certified lender program designed to speed loan approval. Banks that qualify to become certified lenders, those with a history of good management of SBA loans, are promised a maximum three-day wait for an SBA response to loan applications they submit. Certified banks are expected to prepare such thorough credit analyses of business applicants that SBA need only perform brief checks. By 1987, about 30 percent of all SBA loans were processed under the certified lender program, and the certified lenders made 60 percent of all SBA loans (Many loans made by certified lenders are processed either under regular program rules or under the preferred lender program). These percentages have grown every year since the program's inception. While growth of the relative importance of the program is beginning to slow, it is possible that SBA will reach its original target that 75 percent of its loan volume would eventually go through one of the two wholesale programs.[1]

The certified lender program was created in response to a straightforward problem: loan processing delays. During the 1970s SBA's staff had not been allowed to grow as fast as its volume of work. This caused frequent and often long delays in SBA approval of guarantee applications. All participants in the process—borrowers, banks, and SBA staff—complained about the delays. It was feared that they seriously weakened the interest of banks and borrowers in participating. Staff limits, together with participant dissatisfaction effectively limited the maximum volume to which the program could grow.

Instead of expanding SBA staff, the decision was made to delegate greater authority to lenders. The immediate benefits sought from the certified lender program were shorter loan approval times. Longer term benefits would include greater bank support for the SBA program and the prospect that the program volume could grow without costly additions to SBA staff. Once a bank was certified it would have made an ongoing commitment to participate actively, and hence might become more loyal to the program. In short, the problem of processing delays was a clear administrative failing affecting borrowers, banks, and SBA. The primary effect of the solution chosen was to enhance the position of banks in the program.

Experience with the certified lender program to date has shown positive results in achievement of the immediate objective, but some critics claim that the gains are illusory. SBA can show that it has succeeded in shortening approval times. Most of the applications it receives under the program are processed within the specified three days. A 1982 GAO study of this issue concluded, however, that SBA achieved its target primarily by reordering the priorities for processing, between certified and noncertified loan applications, rather than by reducing time actually devoted to evaluating each application. The report indicated that the certified lender program did not actually change the level of review. It concluded that staff savings and overall program performance were minimal.[2] Other than continuing to meet the three-day target, SBA has not developed evidence to counter GAO's charge.

The certified lender program does not materially alter the financial impact of the program on banks, though it makes the loans more administratively attractive. It alters the principal-agent agreement slightly, however, by weakening one of the existing checks on bank decision making. As long as banks have so little incentive to minimize default, the review of applications by SBA provides some restraint, albeit limited. If the intensity of review is reduced from its already low level, higher defaults may occur. In fact, one of the GAO report's main findings was that lenders often "submitted inaccurate, improper or incomplete credit analyses."[3] However, the risk is there that as the certified lender program places more authority in bank hands, it will widen the already substantial gap between the discretion banks have and the consequences they face.

SBA is aware of this potential problem and attempts to prevent it by requiring that certified banks maintain a better than average default record or be expelled from the program. Because of the time between loan origination and the appearance of defaults, this sanction could only be applied after a lag. In practice, lenders come up for renewal of certification every two years. A more immediately effective way to prevent higher defaults would be to reduce the guarantee percentage slightly on certified loans.

On the other hand, the higher level of commitment of certified banks could result in a higher quality portfolio, both because of the commitment and because certified lenders would be further up the learning curve with regard to successful SBA lending. In fact, SBA records show that loans processed as certified loans, and all SBA loans made by certified lenders have a significantly lower rate of purchase than loans made under the regular program. Raw purchase rates for loans made between 1983 and June 1987, were 7.8 percent for certified loans, 9.5 percent for loans made by certified lenders, and 14.0 percent for loans made by noncertified lenders (by number of loans, not adjusted for aging of portfolio).[4] The certified loans also tended to involve smaller losses for SBA, despite their initial slightly larger average size.

The certified lender program takes advantage of the fact that the bulk of SBA loans are concentrated in a relatively small number of banks. Only the more active users would be eligible to become certified. In light of this distinction, SBA's target of converting 75 percent of its loans to certified or preferred lenders raises an interesting question about the future of bank participation. In 1983, the loans at the 75th percentile (ranked by bank portfolio size) were held by banks with only seven or eight loans. Presumably SBA would not wish to certify banks whose participation was as low as this. Therefore, one of the major effects of a fully expanded program, which already appears to be occurring, is to concentrate the loans among a far smaller number of banks than SBA has traditionally used. There are about 650 certified lenders, who account for 60 percent of all SBA loans.

Preferred Lender Program

Taking the certification approach a significant step further, in 1982 SBA began the preferred lender program. The lenders designated preferred are given authority to make SBA-guaranteed loans without prior review by SBA, in return for accepting a lower guarantee percentage (75 percent) and greater liquidation responsibility. In order to qualify as a preferred lender, banks must have demonstrated competence as a certified lender. Most preferred lenders make loans under both programs. When the loan officer feels that a loan requires a higher guarantee, a preferred lender may submit it as a certified or a regular loan. During 1987, there were about 150 preferred lenders, and 8.1 percent of all SBA loans (by dollar amount) were made under the terms of the preferred lender program.

The concept of allowing banks to approve guarantees without prior review by the guarantor, and to liquidate the loans that default is not new. It is used successfully by a large percentage of loan guarantee programs worldwide.

Preferred lenders was intended originally to increase the volume of the SBA loan program. The Small Business Committee on Capital Access stated that, "a major shortcoming of the existing SBA guaranteed loan program has been its inability to attract large scale participation by major lenders."[5] It recommended that "a new guaranteed lending program is needed to lure large sums from major financial institutions."[6] Because the preferred lenders program does away with SBA credit reviews entirely, it offers greater SBA staff savings than the certified lenders program, and this, too, would contribute to greater volume. Of course, in an era of low legislated limits on loan volume, the increase would remain only potential. However, banks and SBA would be poised for expansion, should it be allowed.

The two main features of preferred lenders that differ from its sister program are that SBA does not review individual loan applications before approval, and that banks receive only a 75 percent guarantee. While the certified lender program does little to change the way a bank perceives SBA loans, the preferred lender program changes bank costs and returns, and therefore bank responses, significantly. The lack of prior loan approval would cut the administrative cost of making a loan, while the lower guarantee percentage would raise expected default costs. The earlier discussion of bank returns and incentives can suggest how banks are likely to balance these two features. The administrative cost of making an SBA loan under the preferred lender program would be virtually the same as the cost of making a private loan. Under this circumstance, banks would find it more advantageous to issue guarantees on loans that they would have made even without the guarantee. The percentage of all SBA loans that are duplicative would increase. Thus, the preferred lender program would not be compatible with a strategy for increasing the net external benefits of borrowers. To know more about this, SBA should analyze the characteristics of borrowers and credit terms of preferred loans in comparison to those of the regular program.

The reduction in guarantee percentage would also lead banks toward safer loans. According to the model of returns to banks presented earlier, a reduction of the guarantee from 90 percent to 75 percent would lead to a decrease in returns of 1.9 percent. In order to make up for that decrease, banks would seek a safer group of borrowers. To make returns equivalent to those they make on 90 percent guaranteed loans, they would have to choose borrowers with a default probability about half as high as the current portfolio. In its initial five years, the program has done at least that well, or better. The raw purchase rate for preferred loans made between 1983 and June 1987 stood at 2.6 percent, compared to 14.0 percent for the loans of noncertified, nonpreferred lenders. This is probably an underestimate of the true default rate among preferred loans, because most of the preferred loans are younger than the loans made by other lenders. However, even if correction for age differences showed preferred loans to be twice as default prone, at 5.2 percent, this would be a substantial improvement over all other groups making SBA loans. It is also clear that when preferred loans default, SBA loses a far smaller proportion of the original principal.[7]

While a reduction in the default rate is desirable, it is not beneficial if achieved primarily by increasing the number of guarantees going to already bankable clients. The best way to protect against such duplication is to charge a fee that makes it unattractive to apply the guarantee to already credit worthy loans. Thus, the combination of the preferred lender program with the 2 percent guarantee fee enacted in 1986 should make for an improved program. As discussed below, the combination is the first step in attempting to make SBA guarantees a genuinely market perfecting program.

THE SECONDARY MARKET

The secondary market program, which has been developed and promoted by banks with the strong support of SBA, attacks a different problem: bank liquidity. Under the secondary market program lenders are permitted to sell the guaranteed portion of any SBA loan in good standing to any investor. The lender and investor agree on the interest rate at which the loans will be sold. This rate is not tied automatically to the original interest rate. After the sale, whenever the borrower makes a payment the lender passes along the guaranteed portion of principal repayments and interest payments at the contracted rate to the investor. The lender retains the unguaranteed portion of the principal repayments, and it retains full responsibility for servicing the loan. As a servicing fee it also keeps the difference between the interest rate it receives from the borrower and the contract rate it pays to the investor. An estimated 15 percent to 25 percent of all SBA loans were sold in 1983. In 1987 this figure had risen to about 40 percent.[8]

This arrangement takes advantage of the special status afforded assets backed by the guarantee of the U.S. government. The investor's asset is a 100 percent, full faith and credit security, with size and cashflow characteristics determined by the underlying loan. The guarantee means that investors need no information about the credit risk of the borrowers, information that is costly to acquire. The risk and expected value of the security are known instantly, at little or no cost. Moreover, ownership of the security entails few costs, as no direct relations with borrowers are necessary. Standardization and ease of ownership make SBA loans attractive to institutional investors like insurance companies and pension funds, and make it possible for the loans to be traded through brokers. The investors most likely to purchase the loans would be those seeking the highest possible income from a risk-free investment, who would be willing to bear the unusual cashflow pattern, irregular size, and low marketability (relative to Treasury bonds) in return for a yield somewhat higher than Treasury bonds.

Sale of the loans is attractive to banks, because normally private bank loans can rarely be sold to the general credit market. Banks sometimes sell private commercial loans, but the market appeal of such loans is limited by their lack of standardization, and by servicing obligations, so that they are usually sold only to other banks.

Bankers who use the secondary market cited income and liquidity as the two benefits they sought most from it.[9] The liquidity benefits to a bank from the secondary market are clear, and the value applies whether or not the loans are actually sold. Banks benefit from the assurance that if necessary they can sell simply by telephoning a securities broker. GAO found that liquidity mattered mainly to the smaller banks, intensive users, for whom SBA loans could be an important portion of the portfolio. When used to increase liquidity, the secondary market in SBA loans exploits a benefit already implicit in the government guarantee, namely that guaranteed securities are easy to trade. In this function, it serves a useful purpose at no added cost.

The secondary market is particularly important for a specialized segment of SBA lenders, the nonbank lenders, who account for about 10 percent of SBA's portfolio. Many of these are nondepository institutions; a few specialize almost entirely in SBA loans. For these lenders, the ability to sell the loans on the secondary market is essential to their ability to make SBA loans.

It is more difficult to evaluate the claim that the secondary market increases income for a lender. Both supporters and critics of the secondary market program often display a calculation that shows it to grant banks an enormous return on the funds they put at risk. Here is a sample of this type of calculation. A bank makes a 90 percent SBA guaranteed loan of $100,000 at 14 percent interest, immediately selling the guaranteed $90,000 on the secondary market. It sells at an interest rate typical for government securities with SBA's particular characteristics, 1.5 percent less than the borrower pays. What is the annual rate of return on the $10,000 of the bank's own funds invested? At the end of the year the bank will have received 14 percent on its $10,000, or $1,400, plus its servicing fee of 1.5 percent on $90,000, or $1,360, for a total of $2,750. Receipts of $2,750 are a 27.5 percent return on $10,000 in one year. If, as is sometimes the case, the servicing fee were as high as 3 percent, the rate of return in one year would rise to 36 percent. Most of the SBA loans sold carry servicing fees between 1.5 and 3 percent.

Promoters of the program offer this calculation to persuade banks to participate, while critics offer it as a shocking example of government subsidies to banks. A critical article stated that this level of return "is one more example of how 'providers' invariably seem to be able to capture program benefits intended for their customers."[10] A report in a banking journal cited in the same article used the calculation to show that the secondary market could turn an SBA loan from "the 'dog' to the 'darling' category of our loan portfolio."[11]

Common sense suggests that something is wrong with this calculation. If banks could earn a genuine 27 percent annual return, SBA would be flooded with applicants, and 100 percent, not 15 to 25 percent of all loans would be sold on the secondary market. The clearest problem with the calculation is its omission of administrative and default costs. According to the estimates of administrative costs made in an earlier chapter, the lender of the $100,000 would face $1,870 in acquisition costs alone during the first year, to which would be added maintenance costs and default losses. None of these are passed to the investor.

To make comparisons more precise, we return to the method of assessing the present values of loans used in Chapter 3 (Table 6.1). In this table only the receipts retained by a bank after a secondary market sale are counted. As before, a present value of 1 indicates that the discounted value of future receipts equals the original principal; however, the original principal in this case is the unguaranteed portion only. The discount rate is the government seven year rate, which averages 3 percent below the SBA rate. The first column is the net present value version of the calculation

Table 6.1
Net Present Value of SBA Loans Sold in Secondary Market, as Percentage of Unguaranteed Portion [a] (seven year loans, 90% guaranteed, 14% interest)

Servicing Fee, Percent	No Cost, No Default	Cost Added b/	Cost and Default Added
0.00	1.08	0.36	0.30
0.50	1.21	0.49	0.42
1.00	1.34	0.62	0.54
1.50	1.47	0.74	0.65
2.00	1.59	0.87	0.76
3.00	1.84	1.11	0.99
4.00	2.09	1.34	1.21

a/ The break even present value is 1.00, or 100 percent of the portion of the loan retained. Thus, the NPV of a $100,000 loan for the lender is $10,000.

b/ Costs are: acquistion, 1.87 percent, initially; maintenance, 1.25 percent annually.

given above. If a 14 percent loan is sold at a 1.5 percent spread, the net present value of the bank's investment is 1.47, ignoring administrative and default costs. At this rate, the secondary market sale is overwhelmingly profitable.

Administrative costs are added in column 2, at the rate used previously. They are sufficient, when set against the small unguaranteed portion, to reduce the return by a substantial amount. Default costs must also be added, as the risk of default borne by a bank is exactly the same whether a loan is sold or not. Column 3 shows the net present value of the same loan if both the administrative and default costs are included. Inclusion of both these costs brings the net present value below the break-even level for all but the highest spreads. Not until the spread reaches 3 percent does the present value of the loan equal the break-even value. This is just as expected, because the earlier analysis found that a three percent spread was needed to absorb default and administrative costs for ordinary SBA loans. There is no difference between loan performance in this calculation and in the calculation that applies to unsold loans. The key point for understanding the impact of the secondary market is that although a bank's revenues are great relative to the portion of the loan it retains, its costs and risks are equally great.

Buyers also sometimes pay premiums, offering more than face value for the loans. Banks reported in one survey that they made a quarter of their

SBA loan sales at a premium. No records are available on the magnitude of the premiums. By way of example, an average SBA loan sold with a servicing fee of 1.2 percent and a premium of 4 percent would equal the value of an average unsold loan. It is likely that some combination of servicing fee and premium makes the return to banks that sell SBA loans about equivalent to those that do not.

If the income stream (net of expenses) is the same for a loan that is sold as for one that is held, why should a bank wish to sell its loans? The answer to this question involves a bank's cost of funds, in addition to liquidity requirements mentioned above. An SBA loan sold on the secondary market is best conceived of as the linkage of two transactions that in normal bank operations are performed separately. In most banks, commercial lending divisions make loans while other divisions raise funds through deposits and borrowing. The top levels of bank management coordinate the overall parameters of financing and lending, but this does not affect individual loans. The cost of funds assumed for most loans is a function of the bank's overall financing costs.

In banking practice, an SBA-guaranteed loan not sold would face the same cost of funds as any other bank loan. However, a loan sold on the secondary market would differ in that it is tied to a specific financing transaction that carries a specific cost of funds. If that cost is below the cost of other loans, the sale would in effect be a cheaper way of raising funds. Therefore, the condition under which it would be better for a bank to sell an SBA loan than to keep it is that the secondary market sale rate is below its general marginal cost of funds.

Secondary market rates to investors for SBA loans are significantly higher than the Treasury rate because of the risk of prepayment and illiquidity. One broker reported that the rate on SBA loans was often pegged to the GNMA mortgage backed securities rate, another amortized security with high prepayment risk. The secondary market rate averaged well above the CD rate for the largest banks. Under these circumstances, only smaller banks with high borrowing costs benefit from the sale of the loans. Banks who borrow to raise funds and whose borrowing costs are high are probably large participants in the SBA secondary market.

The error of those who view the secondary market as an income-producing vehicle for banks is to make an artificial distinction between the portion of the loan sold, defined as the investor's money, and the portion retained, defined as the bank's money. This draws attention away from the real issue, portfolio risk. In one discussion of the secondary market, for example, the following statement appears, "When a lender is able to get a high service fee, it can get its entire investment in the loan back very quickly."[12] This way of viewing the secondary market is so prevalent that it is worth taking a moment to show why it is misleading. The appropriate way to view the effect of a secondary market sale involves not volume of funds, but risk relative to bank equity. Through this route, the central role of the cost of funds is clarified.

None of the funds a bank lends are its own. All are borrowed. In theory, the amount of borrowing a bank can do to fund its lending is constrained only by the risk (in the broad sense: expected value and variance of loss) that accumulates in the resulting loan portfolio. That risk must not exceed levels that can be borne safely by the bank's equity capital and default reserves. As risk accumulates, that is, as the portfolio grows, banks face higher and higher borrowing costs. Eventually this cost and the bank's own standards of safety, will constrain the amount of lending. In essence, loan volume is a by-product of the process of balancing return on equity against portfolio risk. However, in practice, ratios of loan volume to reserves and equity are used to set guidelines for total lending. These ratios are really proxies for the amount of risk in the portfolio. They work because bank loans tend to have similar amounts of risk.

But SBA loans have a very different, and clearly defined, risk. A precise application of the principles would require that a $100,000 loan with a 1 percent probability of default count exactly the same amount towards the limit ($1,000) as a $10,000 loan with a 10 percent probability of default. This is the case for an SBA loan, and the amount of risk borne by a bank is exactly the same whether or not the loan is sold. Defaults can be expected to account for $1,600 of a $100,000 loan, even if the bank only holds "its" $10,000. Income as a percent of loan volume will be higher if the loan is sold, but return on equity will not change. Bankers sometimes speak of using the secondary market to recycle funds. However, a bank's ability to obtain funds for lending should be unchanged by the retention of the guaranteed portion of a loan.

One ambitious claim made for the secondary market program is that it grants small businesses the access to bond markets from which they are ordinarily excluded. This is said to occur because it draws institutional investors into a type of financing they normally cannot provide directly. If it did so, the secondary market would make an important contribution to the credit market-perfecting abilities of the SBA program, since lack of access to bond markets is seen as one of the central barriers.

However, banks already have access to institutional borrowers through the money market, and therefore, the secondary market is little more than an alternate mechanism for tapping that source. Banks can borrow as long as their portfolio risks remain within bounds. The money market is the most important source of such funds, and through the money market banks tap the same kinds of institutional investors they would reach through the secondary market. As long as banks can borrow on money markets their small business clients have access (albeit indirect) to the funds of the institutional investors. In providing a new route of access, the secondary market may induce the funds to flow through different, especially smaller, banks, but it is unlikely to affect the overall volume of funds, which is a function of the amount investors wish to invest, and the range of options available to them. If money and bond markets are basically unsegmented and fluid, they tend to "see through" such financial instruments to the real assets behind them. While the government guarantee would increase the market value of a small business's credit, it should have the same effect whether the loan is held in a bank's portfolio or sold on the secondary market. If some banks act as though their income is higher and their volume of lending greater because of the secondary market program, either the program offers them a cheaper source of funds, or they have some constraints to borrowing on money markets.

This discussion has shown that the secondary market program does not greatly alter the profitability of an SBA loan. It can, however, be important for nonbank lenders and for banks with specific problems, such as liquidity or high borrowing costs.

MARKET-PERFECTING EFFECTS OF SPECIAL PROGRAMS

Each of the three special programs SBA has developed is in keeping with a credit market-perfecting rationale for the program. Each aims to enhance the ability of banks to handle small business loans. Borrowers benefit indirectly: if SBA enhances the banks' capabilities, it is hoped that more loans will be made at slightly lower cost to borrowers. In reference to the certified lender program, the SBA stated, "SBA *must* . . . provide a good climate in which the private sector lenders can and will take primary responsibility for providing solutions to the small business community's problems."[13] A principle cited in several SBA publications is "SBA's role in delivering guaranteed financial assistance to small business must be minimized, while the private lending institutions' roles must be increasingly maximized."[14] The link between these programs and a credit market-perfecting conception of the program was stated more explicitly by the former staff director of the Senate Small Business Committee, when he said that if one believes the credit gap argument, the appropriate position for a Republican should be to increase funding, enlarge the preferred lender program and find other ways of increasing reliance on the private sector.[15]

Each reform program makes some contribution toward improving credit markets, within the context of SBA loans. However, as long as SBA retains the basic framework of the guarantee program as is, the scope of that contribution will be limited. The secondary market program is limited by its very nature. It does improve markets, by fully exploiting the value of the government guarantee. Guaranteed securities are more easily traded than nonguaranteed ones because the security value is known immediately. The secondary market allows banks to profit from this aspect of the guarantee, without additional costs to the government. Although the secondary market is not a magic route to increased small business lending, it is worth continuing. SBA's efforts to improve the program by adding a guarantee of timely passthrough of payments and allowing loan pooling, break down unnecessary barriers further. The certified lender program is a sensible attempt to improve the administrative abilities of both banks and the SBA, and has shown some potential to reduce default rates.

The preferred lender program offers the greatest promise for transforming the guarantee program into a more effective one, and this is largely because of the reduction in the guarantee percentage. Its limitation is mainly the small proportion of all loans that are made under the program. If SBA expanded the preferred lender program to the maximum extent possible, keeping certified lenders as an intermediate step, it would reduce the incidence of default, put more SBA loans in the hands of banks that have a commitment to making SBA loans, and make SBA guarantees more like a true market-perfecting program.

NOTES

1. Small Business Association, *Annual Report, 1981,* p. 40.
2. General Accounting Office, *SBA's Certified Lender Program Falls Short of Expectations*, June 1983, pp. i–111.
3. Ibid., p. ii.
4. SBA, Office of Financial Institutions, internal reports, 1987.
5. Small Business Committee on Capital Access, "Increasing Capital Access for Small Business," Unpublished, October 1982, p. 18.
6. Ibid., p. 18.
7. All figures from SBA, Division of Financial Institutions, internal documents, 1987.
8. General Accounting Office, *Certified Lender Program*, p. 46, and Cynthia A. Glassman and Peter L. Struck, "Survey of Commercial Bank Lending to Small Businesses" (Washington, D.C.: Interagency Task Force on Small Business Finance, January, 1982), p. 97.
9. General Accounting Office, *Certified Lender Program*, p. 94.
10. Harold Bergen, "The Maverick Moneylender," *The New Republic*, February 10, 1982, p. 22. See that article and General Accounting Office, *Certified Lender Program*, pp. 50–53, for displays of similar calculations.
11. Bergen, "Maverick," p. 22.
12. General Accounting Office, *Certified Lender Program*, p. 53.
13. Small Business Administration, "Fact Sheet for Certified Lender Program and Proposed Preferred Lender Program," November 1981, p. 2.
14. Small Business Administration, *Annual Report, 1981*, p. 40.
15. Interview with Robert Dotchin, March 12, 1984.

7 Recommendations for Reform

There is considerable room for improvement in the SBA loan guarantee program. The program of the 1980s is better than that of the 1970s, but high defaults still constitute a major shortcoming. If the SBA wants its loan guarantee program to work better and serve the public interest more clearly, it will have to reduce defaults and their cost.

This chapter recommends specific reforms SBA should pursue. A combination of two complementary strategies is proposed, one to improve management efficiency and the other to conform the program more closely to its credit market-perfecting image. Most of the improvements in management have been mentioned throughout the text when relevant. This chapter assembles the suggestions in one place. The recommendation for SBA's program to move in a market-perfecting direction is based not so much on any judgment about the inherent value of that as a goal, as on the fact that SBA is headed that way operationally, and that its best chance of improving its fulfillment of its fundamental public goals is to focus on credit markets. However, it cannot be stressed too much that a commitment to perfecting credit markets implies a commitment to reduce defaults significantly.

Alternatively, if the large default subsidy is to remain, SBA could focus on the other social goals, and attempt to improve the external benefits its borrowers produce, or focus on minority groups and women. This would probably be more difficult for SBA, as it would imply greater SBA involvement in borrower targeting and selection, a trend SBA has been working against for several years. Nevertheless, recommendations to improve net borrower benefits are discussed in this chapter.

Whichever of these ultimate goals SBA selects, it should definitely choose to focus on one, rather than drift along attempting to serve all. The type of program that would fulfill the credit market-perfecting goal well is very different from the type of program that would generate a large net benefit by borrowers.

The likelihood that either course could be chosen will be constrained by the political forces operating on the program. The last section of this chapter comments on their likely effects.

IMPROVING MANAGEMENT EFFICIENCY

The management reforms that have been noted throughout the previous text can be classified into four areas, the structure of the SBA-bank relationship, management of defaults, budget and financial control, and use of program information.

Structure of the SBA-Bank Relationship

The single most important area for management reform is the incentive structure SBA offers banks, and the most important element within that area is the rate of guarantee coverage. SBA has already made significant steps to improve, by selectively lowering the guarantee percentage. More is needed, however.

Prior to 1986, SBA's legislation stated that any loan of less than $100,000 must receive a 90 percent guarantee. For loans above that amount, the guarantee could be lower, but in practice, SBA offered 90 percent guarantees in most cases, exceptions being loans near its maximum limits, and preferred lender loans. In 1986 Congress passed new, and strange, legislation regarding guarantee coverage. For loans up to $155,000 (about the program average), the minimum guarantee percentage would be 90 percent, except for preferred lender loans. For larger loans, the guarantee was required to range between 70 percent and 85 percent. In other words, up to $155,000, there is a 90 percent floor, which changes at $155,001 to an 85 percent ceiling. This law was evidently the result of a compromise between two factions, neither of which wanted to lose ground. On the whole, the rule is an improvement over the one it replaced, as it means that half of all SBA loans, by dollar volume, will carry guarantee percentages that give banks a greater stake in default costs. Congress should take the next step of extending the 70 to 85 percent range to the entire program. (See Figure 4.1 for an estimate of the effect of this change on default rates.) To do so will be a difficult step, as both lenders and borrowers oppose reductions in the guarantee rate, and will offer dire predictions of the consequences. However, Congress should rest assured that the most likely consequence is a significant reduction in the default rate. There may be some reduction in bank participation in the program, but at rates of 80 to 85 percent, if no source of higher guarantees is available, the reduction should be of minor proportions.

Improved default performance has already been demonstrated in the initial performance of the preferred lender program. SBA should study defaults among preferred loans more closely to be sure that the initial indications are correct. If, on closer inspection, it is confirmed that defaults are much lower, SBA should redouble its efforts to expand the preferred lender program. Evidence that a 75 percent guarantee brings lower defaults is the strongest possible argument in favor of reducing the guarantee for the regular portion of the program.

Moreover, if the guarantee percentage stood at 80 to 85 percent for the program as a whole, demand for the preferred lender program would probably increase. Until 1986, banks were faced with the choice of a 90 percent guarantee with SBA approval versus a 75 percent guarantee without it. Many chose to bear with SBA processing in order to obtain the higher guarantee. As the guarantee falls to 85 or 80 percent, the relative benefit of submitting a loan to SBA approval will go down, making preferred loans a more frequent choice.

As the guarantee percentage falls, particularly under preferred lenders, which has so few administrative costs, the possibility increases that banks will guarantee loans that would have received credit without SBA help. The guarantee fee is the most straightforward shield against this. In the same 1986 legislation, Congress raised the guarantee fee from 1 percent to 2 percent. While this was done largely as a savings measure, its effect on bank incentives to avoid guaranteeing already fully credit worthy loans is also important.

Since 1980, SBA has been seeking to reduce defaults by administrative means. It has demanded higher standards of credit worthiness and greater collateral from borrowers. Under the Reagan administration the SBA emphasized loan quality, largely by directing its branch officers to apply more rigorous standards when approving or rejecting guarantee applicants. Such a regulatory approach, while appropriate, has a relatively small potential to cause a reduction, however, because it leaves intact the basic incentives banks face.

SBA is trying to improve not only its relationship to individual banks, but also the mix of banks with which it is involved, through the certified lender program. The goals of changing the mix of banks would be to put more SBA loans in the hands of banks that have developed expertise in handling them and to save SBA staff resources. Between 1973 and 1983 a third of SBA loans were made by banks whose participation in the program was on a very small scale, and Chapter 3 suggested that defaults among this group of lenders was likely to be high. Banks whose participation is more deliberate are likely to be more careful lenders, as lower default rates among certified lenders show. SBA staff requirements can be reduced as the role of its field officers shifts from that of back-up loan officers to that of bank program examiners. While SBA wishes to change from a "retail" to a "wholesale" approach, it has had difficulty in reorienting its field staff. Changing SBA staff from loan officers to bank examiners would require a major retraining effort that SBA has not yet undertaken.

Management of Defaults

While the overall incidence of default will be determined primarily by the guarantee percentage, it should be possible for SBA to reduce the cost of default somewhat by improved management. One area where unnecessary costs are incurred is that of loans that default within the first few months after disbursement. Such early defaults or arrearages show that the loans should not have been made. Reducing that proportion will not be easy, because few direct steps can be taken. SBA could at a minimum learn to understand the problem better. One way of doing this would be to study the use of SBA loans to refinance existing debt, both to SBA and to other creditors. If, as is commonly suspected, refinancing is involved in a significant proportion of loans that default early, more rigorous standards could be applied in that area.

A second area of potential improvement in default management is to shorten the length of time loans in arrears remain in bank hands before purchase. The average during the 1973–1983 period was eight months. This is costly to SBA because of additional interest expenses it must cover and because the charge off value of such loans is likely to deteriorate before liquidation begins. One of the easiest ways to shorten the time would be for SBA to designate a cutoff point, say six months, beyond which it would automatically call in all nonperforming loans.

A third way of improving default management is to make increasing use of banks to service and liquidate purchased loans. Banks have better knowledge of and may also have better leverage over borrowers than SBA. There have already been significant moves in this direction. Preferred lenders must liquidate their own loans. SBA should consider incorporating post-default servicing requirements for banks into all loan guarantee agreements, as is done successfully in many other countries.

Budget and Financial Control

The main deficiency in current budgeting for the SBA program is the fact that costs and subsidies are not accounted for at the time when loan guarantees are approved. It was noted in Chapter 4 that the present value of the subsidy, 9 percent plus SBA administrative costs, should be the basis for appropriations of budget authority to the program. This would not only put SBA on an equal footing with competing direct expenditures programs, it could also help emphasize the need to contain defaults at a reasonable level; if SBA was forced to seek a supplemental appropriation, it would have to explain why defaults were higher than expected.

SBA could take this approach a step further by contracting with a private insurance company to cover default costs. The use of private insurance companies has the potential to improve accountability and, if properly designed, program management. SBA loans are an insurable risk. Even though they default frequently, it is possible to estimate the value of a pool of SBA loans, and the variance of that value, fairly closely. Under this option, SBA would auction to the lowest bidders the rights to provide loan insurance to its eligible borrowers. SBA would pay whatever premiums were asked. Insurance companies could easily develop such bids. In fact, aside from certain particulars of the contract, the premium they would ask would equal the subsidy. The premium would be high by private standards, but it is the predictability of costs, not their magnitude, that would encourage private insurers to bid, and costs of SBA loans are clearly quite predictable.

At a minimum this arrangement would have the same budget effect as the proposal to base appropriations on the subsidy. It would acknowledge the subsidy value of the loans as a direct expenditure, because SBA would need an appropriation for the premium it paid to the insurers. Any further effect on the program would depend on the depth of the arrangement with the private insurers. If designed properly, the private sector involvement could bring about improvements in program operations. Fewest changes would be brought about by an offer for insurers to write a simple policy to reinsure SBA against its losses, without assuming any other administrative duties. This would have little effect on program outcomes. At the other extreme, SBA's role could be turned over to insurers. The private companies would be responsible for approving borrower selection and liquidating loans. SBA would merely monitor the insurers' activities. The introduction of private insurers could change the incentive structure of the program. In general, private insurers would scrutinize risk and follow up collections more diligently than SBA staff, because unlike SBA staff, their monetary returns would vary with their success. Operations could become significantly more efficient. SBA would never own large portfolios of nonperforming loans. Private insurers would also represent a new interest group to support the program's growth.

To my knowledge, the government has never attempted to run a loan guarantee program through private firms. The closest parallel is the emergence of private insurers offering home mortgage insurance like FHA's. The private mortgage insurance firms would be among the most likely to bid on an SBA offer, as they already have much of the administrative structure necessary to carry out the program.

Program Evaluation and Use of Information

This book has pointed out several times that the performance and results of the SBA program have been inadequately evaluated. It is not too harsh to say that it is disgraceful that in SBA's three and a half decades so few systematic, thorough evaluations have been done of the impact of the loans on borrowers. Most studies have been far too simplistic, the usual approach being to ask borrowers how many more people they employ as a result of the SBA loan. GAO analyses, while important, have tended to focus on managerial issues, rather than economic impact. When the U.S. government sponsors similar programs in developing countries using foreign aid funds, evaluations are performed on every project component, every few million dollars, every three to five years. When evaluation is afforded such a high priority and budget for economic development activities abroad, it is surprising that we tolerate so little evaluation of a far more extensive domestic economic development program. A number of other government credit programs show the same lack of concern for evaluation.

Information of an aggregate nature, which exists now, is inadequate for this task. From current information it is possible to learn who borrowers are generally, and which categories of them are more likely to default, but it is not possible to learn about how the borrowers were influenced by the loans.

SBA should commission one or more studies that investigate samples of borrowers in detail. The studies should follow firms over several years rather than relying on a one-time questionnaire. They should concentrate on four areas: first, alternatives to SBA financing considered by borrowers; second, change in performance before and after the loan (such as employment, profits, and sales); third, subsequent credit experience, including development of a customer relationship to the guaranteed lender; and fourth, special characteristics of firms (such as product innovation, or contribution to competitive markets). If possible, control groups of non-SBA businesses should be studied in comparison. Such studies should be undertaken every several years. It will never be possible to reach certainty regarding the impact of loans on recipients. However, SBA could learn a great deal more about its program than it knows now.

Another area that SBA should evaluate more carefully is the financial performance of its portfolio. SBA already has all the data necessary to carry out studies of the financial performance, but the information is not put to sufficient use. The many uses such information has were illustrated in this analysis: to evaluate fulfillment of credit market-perfecting goals, to evaluate program efficiency, and to provide the cost side of a cost-benefit picture. The main challenge SBA faces in using this information is to integrate it into the routine management of the program.

At present, SBA uses the information in raw form primarily to monitor the status of the portfolio in management reports showing what proportion of loans are in normal repayment, liquidation, and other statuses. SBA should develop further applications, using the information regularly to answer the following questions: What are the long-run default and charge off rates? What is the present value of the subsidy? Are banks making a competitive return, or do they absorb some of the subsidy? Without ready answers to questions such as these, basic judgments on program success will be ill-informed. A reasonable standard of governmental accountability would demand that SBA make answers to questions such as these a part of the information it routinely supplies to the public.

Compared to many credit programs, SBA is relatively prepared to use such information because its records are extensive and computerized. It also has a relatively clear set of definitions for delinquency and default, so that losses recorded are probably close to true losses. Using its financial information in these ways would help SBA focus more clearly on efficiency of administration and achievement of ultimate goals.

ACHIEVEMENT OF SOCIAL AND ECONOMIC GOALS

With respect to its ultimate social and economic goals, the SBA program is in a quandary. The significant subsidy for default losses deflates the claim of correcting credit market flaws. The goal of promoting particularly deserving groups or spurring business to exceptional economic growth is undermined by the program's lack of strategic targeting and lack of information about impact on borrowers. At present, the SBA pays the subsidy with little regard for the benefit that would compensate for it. In trying to serve all goals, the program serves none well.

The two major goals conflict because they require different performance standards and areas of concentration. The SBA program's focus on the mechanics of bank operations and relative lack of concern with who borrowers are and how they perform are consistent with a goal of correcting the way the credit market works. But this goal implies a standard of financial self-sufficiency which the program does not achieve. A true credit market-perfecting program would be large, relatively unconstrained, and inexpensive for the government. The subsidy in the program is consistent with a goal of reaching borrowers who are socially and economically productive, if not otherwise credit worthy. But this goal implies a concern with finding especially productive borrowers, or borrowers in disadvantaged groups which the SBA program does not actively pursue. If it pursued high benefit borrowers, the program would need to be small, intensive, and subsidized.

SBA could improve the success of its program by selecting one of the two objectives and moving to make the program consistent with it, while pursuing management improvements. Either model is feasible, but the market-correcting model has the upper hand. SBA already operates the program as if perfecting credit markets were its main concern. All its reforms during the 1980s pushed further in that direction (certified and preferred lenders, the secondary market, the decrease in guarantee percentage for large loans, and the 2 percent guarantee fee). However, several key changes are required before the program becomes a genuine market-perfecting program. Moreover, the success of such a move depends on the existence of a flaw in credit markets that is not certain.

Focus on Perfecting Credit Markets

The chief characteristics of a program that corrects credit market flaws would be (1) no subsidy, or small subsidy with a clear demonstration effect, and (2) broad eligibility, with program size determined by demand rather than by legislated limits. The first is by far the more important. Yet SBA has never adopted the principle of financial self-sufficiency as a standard or even a target for the loan guarantee program. In order to concentrate on perfecting credit markets, it should explicitly make this a target, and work toward achieving it, a few steps at a time.

The ultimate aim should be to convert the program into true loan insurance by requiring users to pay fees that would fully cover the costs of default. Under such a program, no subsidy by the government would remain. Such a move would be based on the premise that if the flaw is within financial institutions, poor credit risk performance by borrowers should not be subsidized. A conversion to this basis would best be achieved by a combination of increasing guarantee fees and decreasing guarantee percentages, until the level of default loss balances against the level of fee income. SBA made steps in that direction in 1986. At its next authorization, in 1989, it should be prepared to assess the outcome of the first step and move further.

When the creation of a small business lending agency was being debated in 1953, loan insurance was offered as an alternative to the administration's bill by at least two small business organizations.[1] Their recommendation was not adopted. Similar recommendations are brought before the committee from time to time, but not acted upon. In 1979, M. P. Koblenski, a former administrator of the SBA, recommended that the program be converted into true insurance.[2] It is likely that the proposal has been presented more recently as well. Thus, while this proposal has followed the program throughout its life, it remains untested.

The potential benefit of moving to true loan insurance is that if it proves workable, SBA would have demonstrated that small businesses can be profitable places to invest term credit. This could change the small business credit market as a whole. There would be a parallel to FHA mortgage insurance, the only U.S. example of a true loan insurance program. Because it did tap an area of market failure, it contributed to a change in mortgage lending practices, and has therefore benefited most home buyers directly or indirectly. Similarly, a successful business loan insurance program could benefit all small businesses in need of term credit, not the small proportion SBA serves now. The housing market has the great advantage over business loans that assessments of value and of individual default risk can be highly standardized and carried out with low cost. Therefore, success for business loan insurance is less likely than it was for mortgage insurance.

The danger of moving toward a fully user-supported program is that if there is no market flaw, actuarial soundness will not be achieved. When banks refuse to serve SBA borrowers privately they demonstrate a belief that they cannot recover interest and fee payments sufficient to cover expected costs and losses. Unless banks have erred in this judgment, or have refused credit for other reasons, a loan insurance program will face the same revenue shortfall. Therefore, a move toward a user-supported program would be risky.

Reasons why a move to true loan insurance might work are the same as the arguments that a financial market flaw exists. Bank preference for short-term and liquid assets is one of the more important reasons. Another is the frequently observed fact that banks do not charge interest rates above a certain level to risky borrowers. Instead, they refuse credit. This may be one of the problems facing SBA borrowers. If so, an initial cost-covering fee would allow the borrower to pay full cost, without the stigma of high interest rates. Neither would monthly payments be increased. This is similar from the borrower's perspective to paying points on a home mortgage. We do not know how willing borrowers would be to pay a higher guarantee fee. Initial reports are that the 2 percent fee adopted in 1986 has not affected demand perceptibly. However, fees of 3 and 4 percent have been sharply rejected when brought before Congressional consideration.

An important implication of converting the SBA program into true loan insurance is that in its most effective version it would have very broad coverage and even fewer restrictions on types of borrowers than the current program. Its success would rest solely on whether it corrects the difficulties banks have in making relatively long-term loans to small businesses. Such a program would attenuate any connection to externalities or specially deserving natures of small business borrowers. By ending the subsidy it would end any necessity for an economic or political rationale to legitimize the subsidy. It would not matter if many of the loans duplicated those borrowers already make. In fact, a more inclusive program would have a better chance of being actuarially sound. The broad coverage under true loan insurance would probably not be achieved initially, as higher fees and lower guarantee percentages would tend to reduce demand by both borrowers and lenders. Attempts by SBA to make its loans more attractive without subsidy should focus first on the preferred lender concept of allowing banks to approve loans without prior SBA review.

Short of a move to full self-sufficiency, the program could be targeted more clearly to gaps in credit markets. Specifically, it could focus on inducing banks to make longer term loans. SBA could establish five, or better six, years as the minimum maturity it would guarantee. This would change the current program only marginally, however. A deeper approach to the same task would be to develop loan guarantee agreements that only cover the later years of the loans' lives, or that cover increasing portions of the loan each year. Institutions involved in the finance of large international projects, such as the World Bank and the Export-Import Bank, have used similar arrangements to induce banks to extend maturities. The advantage of the arrangement is that it leaves a greater part of the risk in bank hands, while still protecting banks against the risks with which they are most concerned. The success of such an approach would depend on the extent to which fear of default in future years is a barrier to extension of credit. The success of the loan guarantee program at extending bank maturities indicates that it is very important. However, the pattern of defaults by loan age (Figure 2.2) suggests that it should not be, as most occur in the second and third year. Adaptation of this approach to SBA would also have to resolve the issue of standardization, as the loan agreements with such clauses are now negotiated on a case-by-case basis.

The SBA loan guarantee program is not the only way to address the credit market imperfections postulated to affect small businesses. Other mechanisms could overcome problems like bank needs for liquidity and the higher administrative costs of small business loans. Liquidity problems could be dealt with through the creation of a secondary market or rediscounting source that would not involve a default guarantee. For example, a Small Business Loan Association could buy small business loan certificates from banks with full recourse (that is, without accepting the credit risk) and finance itself by selling securities in the bond market. This would provide a source of long-term borrowing for banks. This proposal is frequently made by business associations, but has yet to be seriously acted upon. If administrative costs are believed to be the problem, the government could offer a subsidy to cover part of them for the smallest firms. These or related proposals would need further study before it would be clear whether they should be pursued. They are noted here primarily to point out that there are more direct ways to respond to possible credit market flaws than through loan guarantees.

Increasing Benefits Borrowers Produce

The alternative to the market-perfecting approach for the SBA is to allow the subsidy to remain, while focusing the program more closely on high benefit and especially deserving businesses. There are several strategies SBA could pursue if it wished to increase the net benefit from its borrowers. The three factors that combine to produce the program's final net benefits are its costs (largely payments for defaults), the proportion of its loans that are successful incremental credits, and the external benefits produced by its borrowers. These three factors lead to three strategies available to SBA for program improvement.

Reduce Costs by Lowering Defaults. A large cost savings or reduction in subsidy would occur if SBA reduced the rate of purchase and rate of postpurchase loss. SBA's own administrative costs are a second, though less important potential source of savings. The mechanisms for achieving such a reduction, such as lowering the guarantee percentage, have already been discussed.

Cost reduction through lowering the default rate would improve the net benefit picture directly by reducing the total costs to be compensated for by external benefits. It would also improve it by increasing the number of nondefaulting loans. If the bank response postulated in Chapter 4 holds, a 75 percent guarantee rate would reduce the default rate by half (Figure 4.1). The percentage of loans surviving would rise from 76.5 to 88.3, and SBA's subsidy costs would drop from 9 to about 4 percent. If no other parameters changed, this would reduce the required benefit burden per successful, incremental loan from 17 to 29 percent to 6 to 9 percent. This is a major improvement from a 15 percentage point change in the guarantee level.

A caveat is that decreases in the guarantee percentage would likely decrease the proportion of SBA loans that meet the other criterion, that of being an incremental credit. If bank selection standards are raised, a larger proportion of SBA loans will go to borrowers who would have received credit in substantially the same form without the guarantee. With current information, it is impossible to tell how large such an effect might be.

Increase Proportion of Incremental Loans. The proportion of all SBA loans from which benefits can be expected would increase if SBA took steps to diminish the overlap with private credit. The most obvious way to decrease the overlap would be to guarantee more loans to new firms and to minority-owned firms. Any strategy of this sort would, of course, be likely to increase defaults. It is not clear which effect would dominate.

For loans to existing, nonminority firms, avoidance of overlap is more difficult. Loans could be restricted to borrowers requiring credit for maturities beyond those banks could extend, as described above. Given current bank practice, this might mean a minimum maturity of six years.

Target High-Benefit Firms. The targeting of SBA loans to firms with high potential for generating external benefits also offers hope for improving SBA's net benefit level. Firms in the high-benefit category might be new firms expected to grow fast; they might be firms in certain industries; or they might be firms that could meet some standard of labor intensity. Choosing target groups well would require gathering information about the performance of different kinds of firms. The easiest place to begin would be SBA borrowers themselves. Therefore, a first step to pursuing a targeted program would be analysis of the performance of specific groups of SBA borrowers by firm age or industry.

Successful targeting would not be accomplished through set asides that direct a few of SBA's loans to highly specific purposes like the energy program or the handicapped program. Even if the loans under these token programs achieve their objectives, they leave the benefit levels of the bulk of the loans unchanged. It would be necessary for potential benefits to become an integral part of the loan approval decision for every SBA-guaranteed loan. Even if target groups were broadly defined, increased attention to the production of external benefits would improve overall program performance.

A major difficulty with this approach is that it conflicts with SBA's current push towards "wholesaling." A more highly targeted program would require additional SBA staff resources for review of individual loans. It would be difficult for SBA to implement this and at the same time hand over greater discretion to banks. In fact, a highly targeted program begins to sound like a very different program from the SBA loan guarantee program of the 1980s. Moreover, a highly targeted strategy will always suffer from the verification problem, that the economic effect of the loans will be difficult to measure. SBA could use its direct loan program as a targeted program, while moving loan guarantees toward loan insurance. It could also pursue specific goals through other means, as in the case of its Small Business Innovation Stimulation Program, which aims directly at increasing research and development.

PROSPECTS FOR REFORM

The SBA program has always pursued mixed goals as a result of the political forces that shape program policies. The interests of legislators, banks, and small business organizations all favor a program with broad eligibility rules. Legislators favor such rules so that the program will be available to as great a variety of constituents as possible and perhaps to avoid appearing to favor some types of businesses over others. This inclination is strengthened by the influence of banks who wish to retain discretion over borrower selection, and who seek ease and flexibility in participation. Bank interests in having a program that is convenient to use also contribute to the movement in SBA policy toward certified and preferred lenders and the secondary market. All these influences are in accord with credit market-perfecting aims for the program.

These same groups also tend to favor a program that carries a subsidy, or at a minimum, they do not oppose a subsidy. If banks have the freedom to select borrowers with a high probability of default, there will be more occasions for using the guarantee than if they must seek out more credit worthy borrowers. Recipients themselves, to the extent that they have an impact on the program, would certainly not argue for stricter standards or less generous loan terms. Even legislators are unlikely to oppose the subsidy; the cost of the program is small in comparison to the number of clients served, and the budget treatment of loan guarantees described above gives the program further protection. Thus, there is no real constituency for reducing the subsidy, except from those who wish to lower government spending generally.

Because the program as it currently stands is suited to the needs of the groups involved, particularly banks, it would be difficult to redirect it consistently toward one or the other final goal. No strong constituency would exist for conversion of the program to true loan insurance. Borrowers would object to the fees they would be required to pay, and this objection would be transmitted to banks who wish to use the program to attract customers. The small budgetary savings would mean that legislators would find rewards largely only in ideological claims they could make about ending unnecessary subsidies.

A similar problem confronts attempts to reduce the guarantee percentage. Such a reduction would make the program less attractive to banks without increasing its value to any balancing group. A strategy of shifting guarantee coverage toward the longer maturities may be more acceptable. It would not diminish the usefulness of the program to banks because help with longer maturities is one of their main reasons for seeking the SBA guarantee. One way of increasing political acceptance of a full-fledged credit market-perfecting approach would be to insure that a revised program would be useful and available to a larger proportion of small businesses than are the current guarantees.

The idea that the program can and should work toward financial self-sufficiency could be important in motivating changes toward true loan insurance. Financial self-sufficiency is an appealing concept to people with widely varying political views. It is far more appealing than cost-control, which is as far as the agency has been willing to go to date. Adopting it could give SBA a strong position from which to answer critics, and to develop support among its basic constituencies. SBA could say, "Don't stop us now. We are working towards this important goal. Help us get there." Financial self-sufficiency could also serve as a clear direction for management within the agency. Early results from the certified and preferred lender programs show that SBA can move significantly to lower defaults and increase fees. This should give SBA and its Congressional and business supporters confidence to begin to make financial self-sufficiency the program's next goal. The cost of not doing so is a program that continues to provide a subsidy without providing a clear social or economic benefit.

NOTES

1. National Association of Small Business and Smaller Business of America, Inc., U.S. Congress, Senate Committee on Banking and Currency, *Government Lending Agencies*, Hearings, 83rd Cong., 1st sess., May, 1953.

2. U.S. Congress, Senate Committee on Small Business, *Examination of the Mission of the SBA*, Hearings, 96th Cong., 1st sess., October 1979, p. 66.

8 Lessons for Design and Evaluation of Credit Programs

In this book a framework has been developed for understanding and evaluating the SBA loan guarantee program, based on efficiency criteria and on three types of social goals at which it is aimed. That framework provides a structure for deriving recommendations for program reform. This framework and the types of conclusions to which it leads are highly applicable to other government loan and loan guarantee programs. After a capsule statement of the framework for SBA, this chapter sketches the way it applies to some of the more important U.S. credit programs. The approach not only organizes analysis, it leads to some general conclusions about the uses and design of credit programs.

At its simplest level, the SBA program, or any credit program, can be viewed as the provision of a service to a beneficiary group. While such a view is descriptively accurate, it does not always provide a rationale for the program's existence. If we go beyond that level, to ask why the government should provide such a service, the answer invariably appeals to one or more of these three types of objectives:

1. to assist a beneficiary group,
2. to encourage a certain type of economically or socially productive activity, or
3. to correct for a gap in private credit market activities.

The first of these takes the program at face value. In this evaluation of SBA, this type of rationale is the least important, because SBA's borrowing group is diffuse and difficult to distinguish from nonrecipients. The beneficiary group rationale is used primarily to justify loans to minority-owned firms, a small segment of the program. Serving small businesses is, however, important as the de facto operating objective of the agency.

The second objective looks beyond the borrowers themselves to certain activities they perform. In this view, small businesses only receive government assistance in hopes that it will enable them to be more productive. In other words, while the first objective is concerned with who borrowers are, the second is concerned with the response it induces among them. The third objective is not directly concerned with borrowers, but only with improving the financial system.

Just as each objective focuses on a different point in the chain of outcomes a program produces, each involves a different performance standard. The standard for evaluating the objective of providing a service to beneficiaries is first a political judgment about the worthiness of recipients. Beyond this, the main standard is efficiency. The greatest possible proportion of any subsidy given by the government should reach beneficiaries. Administrative costs of all types should be minimized. The efficiency criterion applies no matter what objective is being pursued, and so carries over to the other two objectives as a minimum standard.

The second objective involves a more rigorous standard: the social and economic value of the response induced by the lending should exceed the cost of the program. A subsidy is given only in hopes that it will trigger actions of greater value.

The third objective entails the most rigorous standard. If the objective is to correct a credit market flaw, then the program's financial results should be equivalent to the results a perfectly operating financial market would produce or require. The distinctive characteristic of this criterion is its limitation to financial results. The credit market correction objective can be fulfilled regardless of whether the loans induce new production by borrowers, or the borrowers are in any way exceptional.

In addition to these explicit objectives, the SBA program is influenced by the implicit objectives of banks, small business, and the program's Congressional supporters. Banks, as the service providers, wish to obtain the greatest possible profits from participating in the program. There is a great deal of overlap in practice between their aims and the types of activities implied under a credit market perfection rationale, and this is probably a major reason for the importance of the credit market objective in actual program operations. However, banks are not concerned that the loans meet that objective's overall financial performance criterion; they are concerned that their participation be worthwhile to them.

The aims of both small businesses and Congressional supporters are more nearly related to the first objective. They wish to see the program serve as many beneficiaries as possible at the lowest cost. Thus, one interest group pulls the program toward one model, while the others pull it toward another, and none of them are highly concerned with minimizing costs or subsidy.

All these objectives motivate the SBA program to some degree. In large part, the poor performance we have observed in SBA's fulfillment of its social and economic goals results from its simultaneous pursuit of each type of objective. This has contributed to a general lack of attention to and definition of performance standards. The suggested remedy stated above is to move more distinctly toward one of the explicit objectives. The chapter asserted that the more clearly the SBA program can focus on one of these objectives, the more successful it will be.

If the SBA program were to be devoted to one of these objectives, it would adopt certain characteristic features. As a credit market-perfecting program it would be self-supporting (unsubsidized), with very broad eligibility rules; it would serve a large number of borrowers; and would require a minimal amount of federal staff involvement. As an externality program, with emphasis on inducing faster growth or more employment from borrowers, it would be subsidized (through default payments). It would focus on borrowing groups readily distinguishable from noneligible groups, both in order to reach high performers and in order to reduce duplication of private sector activities. This would probably mean more federal staff and smaller loan volume. It would also devote attention to ascertaining how borrowers behave after receiving their loans. As a service program, the SBA program would be similar to an externality program, except that its borrowers would be chosen on the basis of different criteria, such as poverty or membership in a disadvantaged group, and their subsequent performance might receive less attention.

APPLICATION TO OTHER CREDIT PROGRAMS

This framework for evaluating the SBA program can be applied to virtually any credit program to provide an organized approach to its evaluation. The review of several important U.S. programs that follows describes each program using this framework. It does not attempt to reach specific conclusions about any of these programs, but to illustrate how the framework developed for understanding the SBA program can be helpful. A major theme is that the most successful programs are those most fully dominated by a single one of the objectives.

Federal Housing Administration (FHA) Mortgage Insurance

The FHA mortgage insurance program has always been clearly focused on improving the operation of mortgage markets. It has the basic characteristics of a credit market-perfecting program: high volume, broad eligibility, and low (or no) subsidy. At its creation it entered an area where the financial institutions were not working as well as they could, and as a result it has been very successful. Few other government credit programs have discovered such a clear market flaw. A related reason for its success is that it has been actuarially sound. The program began at the same time as RFC, but unlike RFC, embraced the principle of self-sufficiency, by being organized as a mutual insurance program. Excess premiums are, in principle, distributed to policyholders when the insurance coverage ends. Because it has been constrained to the standard of actuarial soundness, it has always had a motivation for improving its own mechanics and responding to changes in mortgage markets.

It departed from this standard in several subprograms during the 1960s when it experimented with subsidized programs to help disadvantaged groups. These programs generally were not successful, some of them causing significant embarrassment to the FHA and undermining the financial standing of the FHA fund. Most of them were curtailed or discontinued.

In response to FHA's success, the private mortgage insurance industry has developed a service similar to FHA's. Therefore, the need for a government program has diminished. FHA's case for continuation rests on its claim that it still serves borrowers at the margin of private acceptability, and is still a source of innovation in mortgage instruments (though the latter is often disputed). The program's actuarial soundness protects it from opposition; as long as there is no cost to continuing it, and as long as demand continues, it is difficult to argue that any benefit would come from ending it.

Veterans Administration Mortgage Insurance

This program is like FHA's program in all but two respects: it offers easier terms (no downpayment) and is open only to veterans. It attaches the objective of providing a service to a specially deserving group to the FHA's credit market-perfecting objective. Its easier terms result in a subsidy. This program has been successful despite pursuing two aims at once in large part because its target group is so clearly defined. Eligibility tests are administratively simple, and the possibilities of expanding eligibility by changing definitions are limited.

Guaranteed Student Loans

The constellation of explicit and implicit objectives surrounding the guaranteed student loan program is surprisingly similar to that facing SBA. Like the SBA program, the student loan program simultaneously pursues the objectives of inducing a response from borrowers and correcting credit market flaws. The desired response is increased college enrollment. The market flaw is the fact that financial institutions cannot accept the results of an education loan (future income) as collateral, especially given their already high administrative costs due to the small size of student loans.

Therefore, they do not make such loans. Like SBA, the program goes beyond its market-perfecting goal to provide a subsidy, and like SBA, it is not clear that the subsidy will produce the desired effect. Finally, the difficulty in verifying the effect tends to push the program toward simple service delivery to beneficiaries.

In keeping with the market-perfecting aim, the program has very broad eligibility rules, which have generally excluded only families with sufficient income to pay for education expenses directly. Yet in keeping with the borrower response goal, the program contains a substantial interest rate subsidy, in addition to a subsidy for defaults. The total subsidy may be worth about half the original loan principal, making the program far more heavily subsidized than SBA's business loan guarantees.[1] The loans go to a large number of students, but only a few of those students decide whether to attend college on the basis of the loans. One study concluded that less than 25 percent do.[2] A result of providing a subsidy to such a broad group is a very costly program.

In another similarity to SBA, the program is strongly influenced by the implicit goals of a group other than the stated beneficiary; in this case it is colleges and universities. Under their influence and that of recipients themselves, the guaranteed student loan program has become in effect a subsidy to colleges (particularly private ones) and college students, rather than either a way of alleviating a credit market constraint or a program targeted at increasing student enrollment. It is on the verge of being considered an entitlement. There has been great resistance to proposals to place the focus back on the original objectives. The subsidies are too attractive to be given up easily, though some reductions have been made through origination fees and higher interest rates.

Farmers Home Administration (FmHA)

The FmHA makes both short- and long-term loans to farmers for purposes varying from land and equipment purchase to emergency credit. Its loans are subsidized by low interest rates and lenient foreclosure policies. These farm credit programs were originally begun at a time (the 1930s) when the agriculture credit markets were localized and poorly developed. They were originally aimed at low income, small farmers.

At present, the market-perfecting justification has weakened, and targeting has been relaxed, leaving FmHA credit programs with unclear purposes. The size restrictions on eligible farms have been removed. The agricultural credit markets are operating on a national basis now, through private institutions and the government sponsored Farm Credit System. Finally, there is little indication that the FmHA loans actually influence agricultural investment significantly. According to one analysis of the economic impact of FmHA loans, "The implications of their study [a study by LeBlanc and Hrubovcak] are that loan subsidies are a fairly inefficient means of promoting capital investment in agriculture and that the farm loan subsidies should be seen primarily as income transfers."[3] In short, in its routine agricultural credit programs the FmHA has moved away from all three clear objectives, and has become a general farm sector subsidy received by farmers who have difficulty qualifying for credit on commercial terms. As a result, the agricultural credit programs are not highly regarded outside the strong farm lobby that supports them. The sole exception is the emergency credit scheme. Farms that have suffered disasters are probably not adequately served by private markets, so the emergency program has a market-perfecting justification as well as a distributional aim to help an unfortunate group.

The rural housing program of FmHA, although more deeply subsidized than the agricultural credit programs, is more clearly consistent with one objective, to enable low income residents of rural areas to purchase homes. The program provides home mortgages. The borrower's interest rate is determined by family income, and can be as low as 1 percent. The program is a subsidy to a disadvantaged group, clearly defined by geography and income. Alternative ways of helping to provide housing to the same groups would likely be more costly; a loan program requires borrowers to make as large a contribution to total costs as they can. On this basis, it appears that the program is an effective vehicle for accomplishing a distributional objective.

Export-Import Bank (Eximbank)

While the two main programs of the Eximbank, risk insurance and direct loans, are both involved in financing exports, they support very different objectives. The first is a guarantee attached to the loan a foreign buyer uses to finance the purchase of American products. The guarantee comes into effect if exchange rate fluctuations, foreign exchange controls, or political disturbances render the buyer unable to repay the loan in U.S. currency. The objective of this program is clearly to improve on the abilities of private financial institutions. The types of risk involved have been difficult for private insurers to handle. The international economic conditions that create the risks have a strong systematic element across countries; the 1980s have been a particularly difficult time as the third world's debt problems have constrained borrowers in many countries. Furthermore, the government has a unique role because many of the foreign clients are governments or government-owned corporations. Eximbank has not been able to run this program on a fully actuarially sound basis, though borrowers are charged a significant portion of ultimate costs. Eximbank has also attempted to devolve some of the risk onto private insurers through joint ventures. While the program is not fully self-sustaining, its administrators have maintained a clear focus on perfecting credit markets.

Eximbank's direct loans are a far more controversial operation. These loans are offered at concessional rates in order to influence foreign buyers to purchase equipment from U.S. suppliers rather than from suppliers of other nationalities. This objective fits clearly in the second category: through subsidy the program intends to induce the volume of exports to rise. A major area of dispute is whether subsidies are effective at inducing the desired result, and in this question Eximbank's position parallels that of SBA. The subsidy may be given without influencing the foreign purchaser's decision about which country's product to buy. If this occurs the value of the subsidy is split between exporter and buyer, with no change in economic activity. Eximbank attempts to monitor this through annual studies of "additionality," which use a concept similar to that used here of successful incremental SBA loans. Eximbank has very little hard evidence to go on, however, in determining whether any given sale would have occurred without its subsidized loan. Thus, while the objective of Eximbank's program is clear, its success in attaining it is difficult to ascertain.

PRINCIPLES FOR DESIGN OF CREDIT PROGRAMS

As a result of the extensive exploration of the SBA program, and confirmation in the brief descriptions of other existing credit programs, several recommendations emerge about the design of effective loan or loan guarantee programs.

First, a program has the best chance for being effective if it can be focused clearly on one main objective. This can be subsidy to a class of borrowers, a subsidy to induce an economic response, or improvement in credit markets. Credit programs can, under appropriate conditions, effectively support any of these objectives. The important point is that the central objective should be clear. The difficulty in reaching clarity is generally the competing influences of various interest groups.

Second, if the objective chosen is to assist a certain type of beneficiary, the beneficiary group should be readily identifiable. The eligibility criteria should lead to easy recognition of whether a given applicant is a member of the target group. This is a major shortcoming in SBA's case, where the basic target group, small business, is so broad as to include the overwhelming majority of U.S. firms. The pitfalls of a diffuse target group are, on the one hand, lack of beneficiary support and haphazard distribution of subsidies to members (as in SBA), and on the other, pressure for extending the volume of subsidies, resulting in high costs (as in student loans).

Third, the objective of inducing an economic response requires vigilance on two fronts: that the credit given is incremental to what would have been forthcoming privately and that the borrowers are influenced to respond in the desired direction. Again the target group should be readily identified, because it should be clear that private banks do not serve the group (at least on the same terms). The SBA program passes this test in its focus on longer maturities and new firms, but for a large portion of its loans it essentially relies on the word of the banks.

In a credit program aimed at inducing a social or economic response, there are so many ways in which highly fungible credit assistance can go astray that assurance of inducing the intended response is not a trivial matter. The linkage from credit assistance to the desired response should be clear. Measurement of the response should be integrated into performance standards and monitored throughout the program's life. If this is lacking, as it is to varying degrees in the case of SBA, student loans, FmHA farm credit, and Eximbank direct loans, the program tends to become a generalized subsidy to beneficiaries. In fact, of the three objectives, inducing an economic response is probably the most difficult to achieve, both because of the lack of verification possible and because of pressure from beneficiaries and service providers simply to receive subsidies. Of the major federal loan programs, none of the most successful have this as their primary objective.

This observation is particularly important with regard to economic development programs, at all levels of government. The business development programs that use credit as an assistance mechanism all fall into the group of programs that attempt to induce an economic response. All face the same difficulties in obtaining and verifying that response that SBA faces. In a country such as the United States, with fully developed financial markets, credit-oriented economic development is not likely to have a major impact. In developing countries, which lack sophisticated financial systems, inducing an economic development response through the provision of credit is far more likely to succeed.

Fourth, if the purpose is to correct a failing in the credit market, the standard of self-sufficiency should be adopted from the start, and held to as closely as possible. As long as the standard is maintained, eligibility rules can be broadened, and in fact usually should be broadened to establish a more smoothly functioning market. The standard of self-sufficiency provides both protection against political opposition, and an incentive for efficient operations.

Finally, under any of these objectives, the incentives facing private institutions drawn into the program as service providers should match the objectives of the program as closely as possible. This generally means that they should share to a significant extent in program risks. If these principles were followed in the design of each government credit program, more efficient and effective programs would result.

NOTES

1. Barry P. Bosworth, Andrew S. Carron, and Elisabeth H. Rhyne, *The Economics of Federal Credit Programs* (Washington, D.C.: The Brookings Institution, 1987), p. 149.
2. Ibid., p. 149.
3. Ibid., p. 120.

Appendix: Methods and Results of Analysis of SBA Loan Data

This appendix describes the analytic methods used to generate the results discussed in Chapters 2 through 4, which form the basis for many of the major conclusions of the book. It also presents many of the findings, in relatively raw form.

The analysis consisted of four phases. The appendix is divided into four sections, each covering one of these phases: (1) the life cycle model, (2) regressions of SBA defaults against economic indicators, (3) the model of the value of purchased loans, and (4) calculation of the present value of SBA loans.

The same data was used for phases 1, 2, and 4. This was a file of loan histories extracted from SBA's Loan Accounting System. It included all fixed rate loans disbursed from January 1973 to March 1983, recorded in SBA's computer system. The file contains over three-quarters of all the loans SBA guaranteed during that period. Coverage is most complete for 1973 through 1980. During 1981 through 1983 variable rate loans began to appear in the SBA portfolio in more than token amounts, and some 1982 and 1983 loans may not yet have been recorded on the SBA system when the data set was produced in September 1983.

Six maturity categories were studied: one, five, seven, ten, fifteen, and twenty year loans. Results were calculated for each group separately; then a weighted average provided programwide results. These groups make up the vast majority of loans SBA guarantees. Five, seven, and ten year maturities are the most frequent. One, fifteen, and twenty year loans are infrequent, but were included so that the full range of SBA maturities would be covered. The total data set consisted of 120,052 loans.

LIFE CYCLE MODEL OF SBA LOANS

Once a bank disburses a guaranteed loan it remains in bank hands until one of three events occurs: full repayment at stated maturity, full repayment before the stated maturity (prepayment), or purchase by SBA at the request of the lender upon borrower delinquency. The life cycle model of SBA loans consists of probabilities that a loan will leave the system by purchase or prepayment at every period until maturity, when all loans still outstanding are assumed to be repaid. The analysis uses a hazard model, designed to plot the transition of a population from one status to another over time. Two parallel models, one for purchase and one for prepayment, are combined to calculate the final disposition of the loans. Each has the following form:

$$p_{ij} = m + a_i + b_j + e_{ij} \text{ for } i = 1 \text{ to } I$$
$$j = 1 \text{ to } J$$

p_{ij} = probability of purchase (prepayment) of a loan of age i in calendar period j.
m = mean probability across all ages and calendar periods.
a_i = effect on probability from a loan being i months old.
b_j = effect on probability from being in calendar period j.
I = number of months to maturity.
J = number of calendar periods of observation.

The probability of purchase (prepayment) consists of a mean, an effect related to loan age and one related to general conditions affecting the program at specific times. The variables for each loan are constructed from four items: maturity, date of disbursement, date of purchase, and date of full repayment.

The dependent variable, p_{ij}, is constructed by dividing the number of loans of a given age that are outstanding at a certain time by the number of such loans that default (or, are prepaid).

$$p_{ij} = d_{ij}/n_{ij}$$

d = number of defaults (prepayments).
n = number of loans outstanding.

The probability is, therefore, conditional on the loans having reached the period in question, and is independent of the past history of the loans. It represents the underlying propensity of the loans at each age/calendar time period to be purchased.

The dependent variable has in principle as many observations as there are age/calendar time combinations. For seven year loans this would be 84 age months times 123 calendar months, for a total of 10,332 observations. However, some of the observation cells are necessarily empty. Observations begin with loans disbursed in January 1973, and therefore, in June 1973 the only loans under observation are six months or less in age. When the empty combinations are subtracted, the number of dependent variable observations falls to 6,804 for seven year loans. Each observation is in turn weighted by the number of loans in it. An individual loan appears in many of the age/calendar time cells. For example, a loan disbursed in January 1973 that defaulted in January 1974 would appear twelve times. The weighted total of observations far exceeds the actual number of loans. There are, in fact, 2 million loan-months studied for seven year loans. Because of the length of the observation period, the last years of the fifteen and twenty year loans are not included in the model, which stops at age 123, ten years and three months.

The age and time parameters are estimated as a series of dummy variables, one for each possible age, k, and one for each calendar period, 1. Seven year loans have 84 plus 123 or 207 independent variables. Two dummies are omitted so that the model will not be overdetermined. For each p_{ij} all of the dummies but two will have zero value, the age dummy for $i = k$ and the calendar time dummy for $j = l$.

It is assumed that the age effects and the calendar time effects are independent. However, the lack of symmetry in the observation matrix prevents this from being entirely true: observations of early years are all of young loans, and observations of aged loans are all based on events in the later years. The need to correct for this interconnection requires that the parameters be estimated together, using weighted least squares. If they had been truly independent a much simpler arithmetic calculation would have sufficed. The equation estimated using dummies is:

$$P_{ij} = \sum_{k=1}^{I} AK_{ij}a'l + \sum_{l=1}^{J} Bl_{ij}b'k + e_{ij}$$

Analysis of the resulting coefficients can show the effect of age on probabilities of default, holding the effects of time constant, and separately, the effects of calendar time periods on default, holding age constant, as displayed in Chapter 2.

Point of Reference

As estimated, the model results in the choice of an arbitrary age-calendar time cell as the constant term, or point of departure. The coefficients of all other variables are defined with reference to that cell. The choice of reference period is arbitrary and does not affect measurement of the relative changes in default level from period to period.

However, when the model is used to isolate the effects of age from those of calendar time so each can be viewed separately, the choice of reference period is important. If the age or time parameters are viewed alone, the choice of reference point shifts the parameters up or down by a constant factor, which in turn affects the calculation of the long-run rate of purchase so important in evaluating the SBA program. The estimated long-run purchase probability would be far higher if August 1975 were chosen as the reference cell than if August 1979 were selected.

A sensible point of reference must be chosen. The point chosen here is the weighted grand mean, the overall probability of default across all cells, weighted by the number of loans in each of these cells.

$$m = \sum_{i=j} d / \sum_{i=j} n$$

This choice has the virtue that the weighted average of all the age coefficients, and of all the time coefficients, will equal the average probability of default in the data set as a whole. The overall performance of the decade is taken as the reference. The a' and b' parameters are rescaled by adding a constant that will result in age parameters that deviate around the grand mean and time parameters that deviate around the same mean.

Results

Summary statistics for the models are shown in Table A.1. The r-squared and f-statistics are extremely high in all cases. This is not surprising given that the variables used are more descriptive than explanatory. The coefficients for each of the models have t-statistics well above the 5 percent level, on average, with the exception of twenty year loans (due to thin data in many of the cells). The coefficients estimated, scaled by the grand mean, are presented in Tables A.2 through A.5.

ECONOMIC INDICATORS AND THE PROBABILITY OF PURCHASE

This section documents the results of regressions linking changes in the probability of default of SBA loans over time to variations in economic conditions. Several economic variables were tested, including indicators of growth and recession, interest rates, and financial sector variables. These explanatory variables were also tested in real, change, and lagged form. In most cases, however, correlations were higher and regression results better when the original variable was used. The most effective forms of the dependent variables were six-month moving averages. The moving averages smooth out variation due to monthly reporting quirks, and incorporate the effects of the conditions over a longer period. At the same time, they increase serial correlation in the regressions (see below).

The procedure used was stepwise regression, beginning with one variable and adding additional ones, based on their contributions to the r-squared statistic. Many of the variables tested are highly correlated with each other, as they measure slightly different aspects of the business cycle. The estimation process is one of choosing variables that measure the most impor-

Table A.1
Summary Statistics for Models of Loan Purchase and Prepayment

Statistic	MATURITY					
	One	Five	Seven	Ten	Fifteen	Twenty
PURCHASES						
Number of loans	2,511	24,516	46,096	34,648	9,980	2,301
Percent of all loans	2.1%	20.4%	38.4%	28.9%	83.1%	19.2%
Loan-months ('000)	30	961	1,966	1,680	512	120
No. of cells	1,404	5,580	6,804	7,560	7,565	7,565
Mean probability	0.588%	0.558%	0.480%	0.403%	0.251%	0.296%
R-squared	0.96	0.996	0.998	0.997	0.987	0.96
F-statistic a/	229	7425	16058	10090	2277	720
T-statistics:						
Age, mean	12.24	24.03	32.43	18.99	4.84	0.22
Time, mean	3.70	32.12	85.39	60.15	27.54	2.93
PREPAYMENTS b/						
Loan-months ('000)	21	577	1,365	1,132	374	101
No. of cells	612	3,060	4,212	4,968	4,973	4,973
Mean probability	0.755%	1.045%	0.744%	0.501%	0.271%	0.245%
R-squared	0.98	0.998	0.999	0.998	0.99	0.97
F-statistic a/	176	10974	30623	18133	3601	1176
T-statistics:						
Age, mean	10.64	27.96	38.85	11.63	3.37	0.72
Time, mean	4.91	36.69	64.13	54.10	21.31	18.04

a/ Critical value, 1.2

b/ Prepayments recorded from January 1979.

tant aspects with least interference from other variables. Equations were judged on the basis of both high r-squared and economy in number of variables included. Thus, if a variable increased the r-squared by only one or two points it was discarded, even if its t-statistic was minimally significant.

Of several variables tested alone, only industrial production and unemployment explained a significant proportion of the variation in default probability for seven year loans (Table A.6, equations a-d). Industrial production, with an r-squared of .57 and a t-statistic of -12.5, is clearly an excellent predictor. Several variables were tested in combination with industrial production (equations e-h). Of these, the variable raising the r-squared most was the volume of commercial and industrial loans (C&I loans) outstanding at major commercial banks. Additional variables were tested (equations i-j), but none added appreciably to the r-squared generated by industrial production and C&I loans. Not shown are tests of other interest rates, which were essentially the same as those using the certificate of deposit rate, and interest rates in combination with other variables, which did not yield higher r-squareds.

Table A.2
Probability of Purchase, by Loan Age (quarterly, in percent)

Age of Loans	One	Five	MATURITY Seven	Ten	Fifteen	Twenty
	0.039	-0.181	0.104	0.168	0.128	-0.069
	0.825	0.282	0.333	0.334	0.200	0.118
	2.518	1.095	1.001	0.892	0.444	0.332
1 Year	5.131	2.060	1.535	1.451	0.865	0.402
		2.423	1.908	1.873	1.030	1.001
		2.450	2.168	1.984	1.129	0.893
		2.445	2.388	1.934	1.327	1.136
2 Years		2.690	2.286	2.039	1.347	1.127
		2.433	2.363	1.986	1.202	1.331
		2.239	2.150	1.989	1.071	0.839
		2.111	2.090	1.588	1.115	1.052
3 Years		2.112	1.936	1.548	1.023	0.992
		1.749	1.662	1.419	1.031	1.284
		1.518	1.499	1.425	0.720	1.416
		1.464	1.270	1.111	0.959	1.116
4 Years		1.528	1.232	1.129	0.751	1.028
		1.384	1.179	1.049	0.736	1.238
		1.211	1.030	1.055	0.644	1.039
		1.207	0.950	1.036	0.470	1.209
5 Years		1.218	1.023	0.910	0.726	1.442
			0.748	0.920	0.694	0.871
			0.774	0.609	0.296	0.667
			0.517	0.565	0.676	1.235
6 Years			0.598	0.628	0.243	0.523
			0.373	0.597	0.227	0.741
			0.507	0.460	0.252	1.176
			0.483	0.379	0.206	2.627
7 Years			0.299	0.358	0.286	0.156
				0.339	-0.036	2.959
				0.126	0.017	-0.036
				0.073	0.008	-0.078
8 Years				-0.009	0.260	3.180
				0.026	0.163	-0.216
				0.172	-0.180	-0.140
				0.140	0.052	-0.072
9 Years				-0.262	-0.076	0.027
				-0.296	-0.415	4.126
				0.114	0.072	0.247
				0.192	-0.053	0.091
10 Years				-0.298	-0.509	0.224
					-0.703	0.031

For five year loans, the very high correlation between default probabilities and industrial production means that it alone is sufficient to generate an r-squared of .83 (Table A.7, equation a). The coefficient on that variable is twice as big as for seven year loans, showing that five year loans are twice as sensitive. The CD rate is more important than it was for seven year loans (equation b). The addition of this and a time marker to industrial production helps push the r-squared slightly higher, and can yield significant

Table A.3
Probability of Prepayment, by Loan Age (quarterly, in percent)

Age of Loans	One	Five	Seven	Ten	Fifteen	Twenty
	-0.237	0.152	0.097	0.011	0.029	0.043
	0.426	0.175	0.128	0.082	0.084	-0.165
	3.163	0.591	0.329	0.234	0.085	-0.023
1 Year	5.123	1.103	0.671	0.506	0.420	0.380
		1.288	0.936	0.721	0.417	0.377
		1.445	1.283	0.814	0.603	0.577
		2.129	1.509	0.943	0.807	0.716
2 Years		2.296	1.771	1.038	0.779	0.529
		2.497	1.944	1.150	0.905	0.818
		3.106	1.936	1.307	1.055	0.848
		3.168	2.150	1.413	0.853	0.928
3 Years		3.877	2.283	1.476	0.995	0.861
		3.869	2.755	1.299	0.776	1.344
		4.214	2.535	1.374	1.043	1.031
		4.990	3.032	1.611	1.141	0.690
4 Years		6.358	3.267	1.992	1.029	0.939
		7.509	3.746	2.143	1.204	1.729
		8.334	4.159	2.326	0.985	1.381
		9.796	4.075	2.216	0.981	0.838
5 Years		7.367	4.071	2.224	1.130	0.711
			4.315	2.203	1.108	0.266
			4.542	2.367	1.217	0.679
			4.968	2.452	1.308	1.464
6 Years			5.492	2.512	1.085	0.881
			6.187	2.763	1.295	0.415
			6.399	2.497	1.496	0.957
			7.965	2.573	0.586	-0.193
7 Years			6.604	2.144	0.702	-0.325
				2.381	1.068	0.059
				2.835	0.883	-0.019
				2.961	1.311	0.144
8 Years				2.994	1.151	0.162
				3.439	0.636	-0.111
				4.608	1.702	0.173
				5.169	1.460	0.041
9 Years				4.764	1.636	4.147
				4.442	1.058	0.190
				5.581	1.645	-0.025
				5.764	1.229	0.164
10 Years				7.301	1.106	-0.258
					-0.567	-1.073

t-statistics, but most of the explanatory power comes from industrial production (equation c).

The regressions for ten year loans show much the same results as those for seven year loans. The combination of industrial production and C&I loans produces an r-squared of .85 (equation d). In this case, however, more of the explanatory power comes from the C&I loans than from industrial production (equation e). Unemployment is a good predictor by

Table A.4

Cumulative Probability of Purchase, by Loan Age (quarterly, in percent)

Age of Loans	One	Five	MATURITY Seven	Ten	Fifteen	Twenty
	0.039	-0.181	0.104	0.167	0.128	-0.069
	0.857	0.100	0.435	0.500	0.327	0.049
	3.261	1.178	1.421	1.380	0.768	0.380
1 Year	7.693	3.153	2.904	2.788	1.617	0.780
		5.395	4.699	4.562	2.614	1.762
		7.575	6.673	6.391	3.689	2.625
		9.658	8.768	8.122	4.928	3.705
2 Years		11.841	10.692	9.894	6.160	4.757
		13.721	12.600	11.567	7.235	5.974
		15.363	14.265	13.188	8.174	6.728
		16.827	15.816	14.443	9.131	7.655
3 Years		18.212	17.194	15.630	9.991	8.513
		19.295	18.325	16.686	10.842	9.598
		20.181	19.303	17.720	11.425	10.764
		20.985	20.098	18.503	12.188	11.665
4 Years		21.763	20.836	19.275	12.774	12.480
		22.409	21.508	19.971	13.337	13.436
		22.923	22.065	20.646	13.821	14.218
		23.386	22.554	21.289	14.169	15.105
5 Years		23.803	23.054	21.836	14.697	16.143
			23.402	22.371	15.194	16.761
			23.742	22.715	15.402	17.228
			23.957	23.023	15.869	18.074
6 Years			24.193	23.356	16.034	18.427
			24.330	23.663	16.186	18.917
			24.505	23.891	16.352	19.686
			24.660	24.076	16.487	21.345
7 Years			24.747	24.244	16.672	21.443
				24.399	16.648	23.260
				24.455	16.659	23.238
				24.486	16.664	23.190
8 Years				24.482	16.825	25.077
				24.493	16.925	24.948
				24.560	16.815	24.865
				24.611	16.846	24.821
9 Years				24.519	16.801	24.839
				24.419	16.560	27.092
				24.454	16.602	27.226
				24.511	16.571	27.276
10 Years				24.427	16.287	27.397

itself (equation f), but does not surpass industrial production in combinations with other variables. In fact, none of the other variables tested were able to yield an increase in the r-squared or strongly significant t-statistics (equations g-h).

To summarize, the basic measures of the level of economic activity, such as industrial production and unemployment, explain most of the variation

Table A.5
Probability of Purchase, by Calendar Time (quarterly, in percent)

Year	One	Five	Seven	Ten	Fifteen	Twenty
73	7.320	1.389	1.179	1.296	0.978	1.034
	1.638	2.225	1.621	1.032	0.619	0.937
	5.232	1.796	1.812	0.958	1.058	0.858
	4.501	3.384	1.557	1.107	0.450	3.273
74	6.232	3.084	1.849	1.010	0.545	0.675
	7.843	3.781	1.469	1.109	0.693	2.544
	6.849	3.135	1.719	1.150	0.410	4.175
	8.141	3.667	2.013	1.115	0.938	0.229
75	9.122	4.465	2.497	1.638	0.311	1.781
	16.603	4.451	2.191	1.714	1.034	4.908
	9.072	2.847	1.580	0.941	0.310	3.169
	10.031	3.120	1.784	1.344	0.731	4.692
76	1.817	2.299	1.247	0.803	0.710	3.105
	8.605	3.149	2.179	1.225	1.018	6.008
	13.222	2.451	1.557	0.987	0.659	1.518
	15.257	2.140	1.452	0.906	0.532	2.259
77	2.429	1.883	1.168	0.815	0.392	1.953
	5.172	1.967	1.466	1.027	0.674	2.032
	3.112	1.758	1.249	0.974	0.660	1.068
	0.925	1.376	1.027	0.865	0.537	1.114
78	1.379	1.463	1.097	0.737	0.450	1.039
	1.617	1.258	1.110	0.862	0.526	1.089
	1.051	1.062	1.046	0.606	0.395	0.641
	0.024	1.096	0.867	0.596	0.333	0.476
79	-0.528	1.269	0.993	0.860	0.448	1.073
	1.650	1.308	1.072	0.987	0.552	0.716
	0.840	0.871	0.863	0.824	0.360	0.521
	0.028	1.066	0.979	0.670	0.421	0.572
80	0.110	0.699	0.757	0.654	0.354	0.311
	2.103	1.927	1.771	1.385	1.003	1.082
	1.669	1.440	1.351	1.238	0.512	0.536
	1.077	1.199	1.294	1.038	0.601	0.780
81	0.115	1.440	1.368	1.323	0.891	0.983
	1.388	1.404	1.415	1.292	0.756	1.2~2
	0.956	1.290	1.352	1.244	0.880	0.999
	1.865	1.678	1.598	1.520	0.950	1.261
82	0.293	1.049	1.328	1.278	0.917	0.546
	2.551	2.339	2.641	2.709	1.564	1.621
	0.609	1.122	1.249	1.218	0.639	0.320
	1.938	2.217	2.313	2.051	1.206	1.089
83	1.288	1.767	2.233	1.705	1.182	0.503

in SBA default rates. Financial variables, notably interest rates, are relatively unimportant.

Early and Late Periods

In order to assess whether the combination of high interest rates with a recession had a different effect on small businesses than more usual eco-

Table A.6

Regression Results for Seven Year Loans (monthly, from 1/1973 to 3/1983, against six month moving average)

Regression/Variables	Coefficient	T-Statistic	R-Squared	Durbin-Watson
a. Industrial production	-0.89	-12.5	0.57	0.19
b. Unemployment	0.048	6.9	0.29	0.11
c. CD rate	-0.0058	-1.8	0.03	0.09
d. Stock prices (lagged)	-0.00087	-1.1	0.01	0.12
e. Industrial production	-1.23	-6.1	0.86	0.62
C&I loans a/	0.0015	15.1		
f. Industrial production	-1.25	-17.1	0.72	0.46
CD rate	0.017	8.0		
g. Industrial production	-1.37	-18.1	0.77	0.40
Time	0.0023	9.9		
h. Industrial production	-0.79	-11.0	0.63	0.32
Inflation (CPI)	-0.84	3.2		
i. Industrial production	-0.99	-11.9	0.87	0.69
C&I loans	0.0026	8.2		
Retail sales	-0.0044	-3.5		
j. Industrial production	-1.19	-13.7	0.86	0.62
C&I loans	0.0017	5.3		
Wholesale sales	-0.0006	-0.6		

a/ Equation selected as best model.

nomic conditions (either high rates or recession, but not both), the time period from January 1973 to March 1983 is split into an early and late period. The dividing point is between October and November 1979, the time from which higher interest rates are said to date. During the early period industrial production is again the best predictor of default, (Table A.8, equation a). Of all the variables tested in combination with industrial production, the CD interest rate produced the greatest increase in r-squared, from .87 for industrial production alone, to .90 (equation b).

During the later period the combination of industrial production and commercial and industrial loan volume produces essentially the same results as for the whole decade, although the coefficient on industrial production is lower, showing less volatility (equation c). In these years, however, unemployment alone is the best predictor, yielding an r-squared of .89 (equation d). All other variables tested added little or nothing to total variation explained, and results for five and ten year loans are similar. The conclusion must be that the relationships between defaults and economic conditions did not change during the decade, and that there is no

Table A.7
Regression Results for Five and Ten Year Loans (monthly, from 1/ 1973 to 3/1983, against six month moving average)

Regression/Variables	Coefficient	T-Stat.	R-Squared	Durbin-Watson
Five year loans:				
a. Industrial prod'n a/	-2.57	-23.7	0.83	0.28
b. CD rate	-0.036	-5.1	0.18	0.08
c. Industrial production	-2.66	-19.5	0.88	0.47
Time	-0.0078	-4.3		
CD Rate	0.023	6.4		
Ten year loans:				
d. Industrial production	-0.81	-18.9	0.85	0.60
C&I loans a/	0.0022	24.2		
e. Industrial production	-0.31	-3.3	0.09	0.12
f. Unemployment	0.059	12.1	0.56	0.23
g. Industrial production	-0.71	-12.1	0.86	0.67
Time	-0.001	-2.4		
C&I Loans	0.0027	11.5		
h. Industrial production	-0.86	-18.1	0.85	0.64
C&I loans	0.0021	19.7		
CD rate	0.0035	2.1		

a/ Equation selected as best model.

Table A.8
Regression Results for Early and Late Periods (seven year loans, monthly, against six month moving average)

Regression/Variables	Coefficient	T-Statistic	R-Squared
Early: 1/73-10/79			
a. Industrial production	-1.21	-21.1	0.87
b. Industrial production	-1.2	-23.8	0.90
CD rate	0.0096	4.1	
Late: 11/79-3/83:			
c. Industrial production	-0.94	-0.52	0.86
C&I loans	0.002	6.5	
d. Unemployment	0.083	19.3	0.89

special effect from the combination of high interest rates and a sluggish economy.

Serial Correlation

The Durbin-Watson statistics for these regressions are quite low, indicating substantial serial correlation. Among the equations chosen as the most appropriate models of loan purchase, noted in Tables A.6 and A.7, the Durbin-Watson statistics are somewhat higher. Serial correlation results in overestimates of the statistical significance of the coefficients. However, in all of the selected equations, the t-statistics are so far above the critical points for the 5 percent level that they would still be significant even if the serial correlation were corrected for.

Serial correlation could be eliminated by the use of monthly data rather than a moving average. A regression of industrial production and C&I loans using straight monthly data for seven year loans yields a Durbin-Watson statistic of 1.95 and an r-squared of .39 (compare Table A.6, equation e). However, this reintroduces a great deal of noise that is not relevant to the association of probability of default with economic variables.

Remaining Questions

While these regressions are useful in showing the strength of the relationship between SBA loan defaults and the business cycle and the weakness of the relationship to interest rates, they leave several questions outstanding. First, why were loans more likely to default during the 1974–1975 recession than during the recession of 1981–1982? Second, why should the correlations between defaults and several variables, including interest rates, differ so much for SBA loans of different maturities? Third, what is the underlying explanation for the significance in the equations of the volume of C&I lending, with its positive sign? Answers to these questions would require further investigation of this data as well as additional information.

PRESENT VALUE OF PURCHASED LOANS

This section describes the process used to calculate the present value of loans that SBA purchases. The results of this calculation are three expected values for each maturity group that represent the value of a loan at the time of purchase, first to the bank, second from the loan itself (as if it were unguaranteed), and third to the SBA. These values play an important role in determining the present value of the SBA portfolio as a whole. They are the means to summarize the costs of default.

For each loan, the information used is: original maturity, interest rate and guarantee percentage, the date of SBA purchase, amount purchased, whether the loan was fully repaid, and for loans that were charged off, date and amount of charge off. In reaching the final values the model incorporates four aspects of purchased loan behavior: the value of payments missed before purchase; the probability that a purchased loan will eventually be charged off or fully repaid; the expected value of charged off loans; and the expected value of fully repaid loans.

Because the values calculated for purchased loans are to be used in calculating the value of the portfolio as a whole, it is necessary to express them in terms compatible with the model of the present value of the portfolio (following section). That model attaches costs of default to a normal amortization schedule according to the probability of default in each period. As it moves, the model keeps track of the amount of principal outstanding. At any given point the model holds as outstanding the principal balance normally expected to remain at that time (which is termed expected balance). If the loan is purchased, however, the expected balance is usually smaller than the purchase amount because the purchase amount reflects the fact that payments stopped some time before. Because of the role of the normal amortization schedule in modelling the whole portfolio, the values calculated for purchased loans are expressed as percentages of the expected balance.

The estimation process shows that the ratio of the value of purchased loans to their expected balance does not change systematically by time of purchase. Among the loans in the sample, the value of a purchased loan was found to be approximately the same proportion of the expected balance whether the loan was purchased after one, two, or five years. This result differed from expectations. It proved convenient, however, in that it allowed a single coefficient to be applied to purchases occurring at any time after disbursement. The variation in actual value comes from the expected balance.

Value of Payments Missed

SBA loans that are purchased remain in bank hands for an average of eight months before SBA buys them. That estimate was made by comparing the actual purchase values to the principal that would have been outstanding at the time of purchase, had loan payments been up to date. By working backwards along the amortization schedule, the time at which payments stopped for each loan can be computed. This calculation assumes that purchase amounts were recorded correctly, and that borrowers make regular payments until a given point and then stop completely.

During this time, banks are losing money in the form of foregone payments. When SBA eventually purchases the loans, the purchase amount covers the guaranteed portion of the principal from those payments and all the interest. Thus, the value of the missed payments is the purchase amount, expressed in full principal terms, less the expected balance at time of purchase.

$$V_m = P - EB$$

V_m = value of payments missed.
  P = purchase amount.
EB = expected balance.

The amount of payments missed is higher for shorter maturity loans, especially one year loans (Table A.9). This is because while the short- and long-term loans miss comparable numbers of payments, faster amortization of short-term loans means that each missed payment is proportionally more costly.

Propensity of Charge Off and Full Repayment

The cumulative probabilities of charge off and prepayment are calculated from the same kind of hazard model used to calculate cumulative probabilities of purchase and prepayment. However, because of the far smaller sample of purchased loans, it is necessary to compute the probabilities on an annual rather than monthly basis, in order to reach defensible estimates by maturity group. The cumulative probabilities by year are shown in Table A.10.

This process takes the portfolio through ten years. At the end of this period, some loans of longer maturity remain outstanding. The final disposition of these loans cannot be assessed directly. However, we can assume that the proportions of loans going into each category would remain the same as at the end of ten years. This would result in an average cumulative charge off figure of 83 percent, after disposition of all loans.

Value of Charged Off Loans

From loans that it eventually charges off, SBA receives some further repayments from borrowers, and receipts from the sale of collateral in liquidation proceedings. Banks only receive the unguaranteed portion of this amount, while SBA retains the rest. Direct information about the amounts is not kept, but it can be deduced from available information. At the time of charge off the borrower has accumulated an obligation to repay that consists of the purchase amount plus the interest charges that have accrued during the holding period. The amount SBA charges off is the portion of that obligation which the borrower did not redeem. Therefore,

Table A.9
Value of Loans after Purchase (to banks, SBA, and in total as proportion of expected balance at time of purchase)

Element of Value	Weighted Average	One	Five	Seven	Ten	Fifteen	Twenty
Value of missed payments	-0.26	-1.49	-0.34	-0.24	-0.16	-0.10	-0.05
Recovery on purchased loans:							
Value of charged off loans	0.24	0.07	0.20	0.26	0.29	0.41	0.44
Value of loans paid in full	1.29	2.78	1.36	1.24	1.20	1.18	1.23
Probability of charge off	0.83	0.88	0.85	0.84	0.81	0.76	0.70
Probability of full repayment	0.17	0.14	0.15	0.16	0.19	0.24	0.30
Subtotal a/	0.42	0.45	0.37	0.41	0.46	0.59	0.68
Purchase amount	1.10	2.00	1.19	1.08	1.00	0.96	0.94
Value to Banks							
Missed paym'ts	-0.26	-1.49	-0.34	-0.24	-0.16	-0.10	-0.08
Purchase am't	1.10	2.00	1.19	1.08	1.00	0.96	0.94
Recovery b/	0.05	0.06	0.05	0.05	0.06	0.08	0.09
Total, banks	0.89	0.57	0.90	0.89	0.90	0.94	0.95
Value to SBA							
Purchase am't	-1.10	-2.00	-1.19	-1.08	-1.00	-0.96	-0.94
Recovery c/	0.36	0.39	0.33	0.36	0.40	0.52	0.59
Total, SBA	-0.74	-1.61	-0.86	-0.72	-0.60	-0.44	-0.35
Total value							
Missed paym'ts	-0.26	-1.49	-0.34	-0.24	-0.16	-0.10	0.00
Recovery	0.42	0.45	0.37	0.41	0.46	0.59	0.68
Total value	0.16	0.00	0.03	0.17	0.30	0.49	0.68

a/ Recovery on charged off loans times probability of charge off, plus recovery on paid in full loans, times probability paid in full.

b/ 13 percent of total recovery on purchased loans.

c/ 87 percent of total recovery on purchased loans.

the total amount of receipts is the difference between full obligations and charge offs.

A simplifying assumption is needed in order to assess the net present value of these loans at the time of purchase. Receipts may come from repayments, liquidation, or a mixture of both sources. The choice of mix for a working assumption does not change the raw dollar amount of receipts, but it does change their timing, and hence the rate by which they

Table A.10
Cumulative Charge Offs by Maturity (percentage of original purchase, by number)

Years Since Purchase	Wgtd. Average	One	Five	Seven	Ten	Fifteen	Twenty
Up to 1	22.9	30.8	33.6	26.5	19.1	8.2	6.3
2	40.7	53.9	55.8	43.7	34.1	21.4	22.4
3	51.7	64.3	63.9	54.0	46.0	34.0	25.0
4	59.7	65.4	70.8	62.3	54.9	42.1	29.0
5	64.6	70.9	75.1	66.1	58.9	46.1	29.0
6	68.4	70.9	77.9	71.7	62.6	48.0	38.2
7	70.8	75.2	83.3	73.1	64.7	50.5	38.2
8	73.5	79.3	85.0	74.0	68.1	50.5	38.2
9	75.5	86.9	85.6	74.0	70.3	50.5	38.2
10	77.7	86.9	85.0	84.2	70.3	50.5	38.2
Final charge offs a/	82.8	86.9	85.0	84.2	81.4	75.8	70.4

a/ After all loans have been disposed of. Assumes ratio of charge offs to full repayments stays the same as at the end of ten years

are discounted. A worst case assumption is used here, which attributes all receipts to liquidations. It is easiest to work with, and conforms to anecdotal evidence that few charged off loans have made repayments while in SBA hands.

Using these assumptions, the value of charged off loans can be expressed as:

$$V_c = P + (IPMT - C)/(1 + r)^{(T_c - T_p)}$$

V_c = value of charged off loan.
IPMT = portion of monthly payment devoted to interest at t.
C = charge off amount.
T_c or T_p = time of charge off (c) or purchase (p).
r = discount rate (see next section).

The average size of V_c for the loans in the sample, calculated according to this equation, ranged from 7 percent of the expected balance for one year loans to 44 percent for 20 year loans. It is not known why the value is higher for longer term loans. Possibly, these loans are secured by collateral of higher and more lasting value.

Value of Fully Repaid Loans

The loans that fully repay can be dealt with directly. It is assumed that after purchase these loans resume their regular schedule at the first payment missed, and continue until they reach the final payment. These payments are discounted back to the time of purchase. The expression for this is:

$$V_f = \sum_{T_s}^{T_m} (PMT/(1+r)^{(t-Tp)})$$

V_f = value of fully repaid loan.
PMT = monthly payment.
T_s = time at which payments stopped.
T_m = time of final payment.

Combining the Elements into Present Value

The elements described above are combined to produce the final value of purchased loans to banks, as if unguaranteed, and to SBA. Banks suffer the initial loss of missed payment before purchase, but the guaranteed portion of this is made up in the loan purchase amount. After purchase, banks get the unguaranteed share of whatever collections are made. The present value for banks of purchased loans is:

$$BPV = V_m + gP + (1-g)(Cp_c + Cp_r)$$

g = guarantee percentage.
p_c = probability of charge off.
p_r = probability of full repayment.

SBA has a large negative outlay when it purchases the loans and then receives all but the unguaranteed portion of subsequent collections. The value (or cost) of a purchased loan to SBA is:

$$SPV = g(-P + Cp_c + Fp_r)$$

The value produced by the loans themselves is the sum of the elements, weighted by the probabilities (Table A.9):

$$PV = V_m + Cp_c + Fp_r$$

METHOD OF CALCULATING PRESENT VALUE FOR ALL SBA LOANS

This section discusses how the life cycle model of SBA loans is combined with the model of the costs of purchased loans to determine the present value of the portfolio as a whole. Again, the value is calculated for banks with the guarantee, for SBA and for the loans as if there were no guarantee.

The formula for calculating the present value of a loan is:

$$PV = \sum_{i=j}^{I} [(PMT - C) / (1 + r + \beta\lambda)_i]$$

PV = present value.
PMT = income received.
C = costs.
r = base interest rate (risk free).
β = risk of the asset.
λ = market price of risk.
i = payment period.
I = period of loan maturity.

In calculating the present value for SBA loans to banks, this formula is altered to incorporate the changing probabilities of default and prepayment throughout the lifetimes of the loans. Because the probabilities determine not only current period cashflows but also the percentage of loans outstanding, incorporation of these probabilities requires that the expected value of the loan be followed period by period.

The expected value of a loan at any period, given that it does not default in that period, is the sum of the monthly payment less costs and the expected value of the loan in the next period, $i+1$, discounted one period. The expected value in period $i+1$ is the weighted average (weighted by probabilities) of the three possible outcomes in period $i+1$: default, prepayment, or continued survival. This can be expressed as:

$$V_{i+1|s} = PMT - C + [\bar{p}_i(V_i|_d) + \bar{q}_i(V_i|_p) + (1 - \bar{p}_i - \bar{q}_i)(V_i|_s)]/(1 + r + \beta_i\lambda)$$

p_i = probability of default in period i.
q_i = probability of prepayment in period i.
$V_i|_d$ = value of loan to bank in case of default.
$V_i|_p$ = value of loan to bank in case of prepayment.
$V_i|_s$ = value of loan to bank in case of survival.

The probabilities p_i and q_i are taken directly from the age model of probabilities described above. The value of the loan given default is the currently outstanding principal times the ratio calculated for the present value of purchased loans, and the value in prepayment is simply the outstanding principal. The value in case the loan survives in period $i+1$ is then given by this same formula, relating period $i+1$ to $i+2$. Thus, the expected value of the loan in each period is linked to the expected value in each following period.

The only period in which the expected value is known with certainty is at the end of a loan's life, when all payments have been completed and the remaining value is zero. In order to find the expected value of the loan at the time of disbursement, it is necessary to begin with the final period and move backwards one period at a time through the loan's life.

The only element in this model that is not available from information developed previously is the risk premium, used to determine the discount rate. The rest of this section discusses how this is calculated.

Beta and the Discount Rate

According to the capital asset pricing model, the beta of an asset is the covariance of returns on it with returns on the stock market, as a ratio of market variance. In order to calculate the beta for a stock it is necessary to have a series of returns on that stock over time. That return is simply the change in stock price from one period to the next, plus any dividend paid. It is not so easy to see what the period-to-period return of a fixed value asset such as a bank loan would be. The comparable measure for SBA loans used here is the change in present value from period i to $i+1$, as shown in the previous equation. This incorporates both the actual payment received and any change in the expected present value.

To calculate beta for SBA loans we need to know the variation of that return over time, or more precisely, the systematic, market-linked component of that variation. The only source of variation in SBA loans is the change in default probabilities, as shown in the life cycle model, and the only portion of that variation that fluctuates over time is the calendar-related portion, which was analyzed in the second section of the appendix. The calculation of beta for SBA loans thus uses the time series of change in default probability from January 1973 through March 1983. As noted above, that series does not relate closely to the stock market (correlation for seven year loans, $-.07$). The covariance was very low, and surprisingly, the sign of the correlation was different for different maturity groups. Moreover, the fluctuation in default probability over time, while in itself substantial, has a small effect on the expected asset value of an SBA loan from one period to the next. In comparison with stock prices, which can vary significantly from month to month, the value of a bank loan, or portfolio of loans, changes little. The lack of variation is almost total when the effect of the SBA guarantee on banks is taken into consideration.

Betas for the six maturity groups of SBA loans were calculated using the model given above as a starting point and according to the principles described in the preceding two paragraphs. The method used was devised by Herman B. Leonard, to whom I am very grateful.

The calculation yielded betas for SBA loans of different maturities in the range of plus or minus .0001 to .004 for banks with the guarantee, and plus or minus .001 to .1 for the loans without the guarantee (stock market beta = 1). It was concluded that these were so insignificant that banks should require no risk premium in the discount rate used to assess the present values of SBA loans. It might be noted, however, that the betas for SBA itself, which holds a distillation of the credit risk of the loans, were far higher, in the range of − .66 to 1.23.

Bibliography

Anderson, Dennis, and Farida Khambata. "Financing Small-scale Industry and Agriculture in Developing Countries: The Merits and Limitations of 'Commercial' Policies." World Bank Staff Working Papers, No. 519. Washington, D.C.: 1982.

Bates, Timothy. "A Review of the Small Business Administration's Major Loan Programs." Washington, D.C.: Interagency Task Force on Small Business Finance, December 1981.

Bates, Timothy, and William Bradford. *Financing Black Economic Development*. New York: Academic Press, 1979.

Bates, Timothy, and Donald D. Hester. "Analysis of a Commercial Bank Minority Lending Program: Comment." *Journal of Finance* 32: no. 5 (December 1977): pp. 1783–1789.

Bergen, Harold. "The Maverick Moneylender." *The New Republic*, February 10, 1982.

Bosworth, Barry, Andrew S. Carron, and Elisabeth H. Rhyne. *The Economics of Federal Credit Programs*. Washington, D.C.: The Brookings Institution, 1987.

Break, George. *Federal Lending and Economic Stability*. Washington, D.C.: The Brookings Institution, 1965.

Cohen, David L. "Small Business Capital Formation," in *Public Policy and Capital Formation*. Washington, D.C.: Board of Governors of the Federal Reserve System. April 1981.

Commission on Money and Credit. *Federal Credit Agencies*. Englewood Cliffs, N.J.: Prentice Hall, 1963.

Deloitte Haskins and Sells. "Report on Loan Guarantee Mechanisms and Other Financial Sector Innovations in Kenya." Unpublished, Nairobi, Kenya, 1985.

Edelstein, Robert H. "Improving the Selection of Credit Risks: An Analysis of a Commercial Bank Minority Lending Program," *Journal of Finance* 30, no. 1 (March 1975): pp. 37–55.

Estefania, J. Ramon. "Financial Status of the SBA 7(a) Guaranty Program: Budgeting, Effects of the Economy on Losses and Alternatives to the Present Program." Unpublished, September 1980.

Feinberg, Richard E. *Subsidizing Success: The Export-Import Bank in the U.S. Economy*. Cambridge, England: Cambridge University Press, 1982.

Fenno, Richard F., Jr. *Congressmen in Committees*. Boston: Little Brown and Company, 1973.

Gentry, Celestea. "Federal Credit Programs: Overview and Origins in the RFC." U.S. Treasury Department. Unpublished, August 1980.

Glassman, Cynthia, and Peter L. Struck. "Survey of Commercial Bank Lending to Small Business." Washington, D.C.: Interagency Task Force on Small Business Finance, January 1982.

Grimshaw, Alan, and Robert O. Edmister. "SBA Default Rates: Selection Bias and Credit Deterioration," *Journal of Economics and Business* 34, No. 4 (1982): pp. 343–48.

Harris, Candee, with Nancy O'Conner and Kirk Kimmell. *Handbook of Small Business Data*. Washington, D.C.: The Brookings Institution, draft, January 1983.

Hillman, Jordan Jay. *The Export-Import Bank at Work: Promoting Financing in the Public Sector*. Westport, Conn.: Quorum Books, 1982.

Hodgman, Donald R. *Commercial Bank Loan and Investment Policy*. Champaign: University of Illinois Press, 1963.

Hudgins, Edward L., and Stephen Moore. "Helping Small Business by Abolishing the Small Business Administration." Washington, D.C.: Heritage Foundation, 1985.

Hunter, William C. "Commercial Bank Behavior Under Risk Insensitive SBA Insurance Premiums." School of Business Administration, Emory University, unpublished. Atlanta: 1984.

———. "Moral Hazard, Adverse Selection and SBA Business Loan Guarantees", in Congressional Budget Office, *Conference on the Economics of Federal Credit Activities, Part 2*, pp. 233–80. Washington, D.C.: 1981.

Interagency Task Force on Small Business Finance (Federal Reserve, FDIC, Comptroller of the Currency, Census Bureau, SBA). *Studies of Small Business Finance*. Washington, D.C.: February 1982.

Jacobs, Donald P. "Business Loan Costs and Bank Market Structure: An Empirical Estimate of Their Relations." National Bureau of Economic Research, Occasional Paper 115. New York: 1971.

Jacoby, Neil H., and Raymond J. Saulnier. *Business Finance and Banking*. New York: National Bureau of Economic Research, 1947.

———. *Term Lending to Business*. New York: National Bureau of Economic Research, 1952.

Jones, Jesse H., with Edward Angly. *Fifty Billion Dollars: My Thirteen Years with the RFC*. New York: Macmillan, 1951.

Klein, Richard. "SBA's Business Loan Programs." *Atlanta Economic Review* 28 (September-October 1978): 28–37.

———. "Financial Results of the Small Business Administration's Business Loan Portfolio." *University of Michigan Business Review* (January 1978): pp. 17–26.

Levitsky, Jacob, and Ranga N. Prasad. "Credit Guarantee Schemes for Small and Medium Enterprises," World Bank Technical Paper No. 58. Washington, D.C.: The World Bank, 1987.

Penner, Rudolph G., and William L. Silber. "The Interaction between Federal Credit Programs and their Impact on the Allocation of Credit." *American Economic Review* 63 (December 1973): 838–52.

Robson Rhodes, Chartered Accountants. "A Study of Businesses Financed under the Small Business Loan Guarantee Scheme." London: U.K. Government, Department of Trade and Industry, 1984.

Saulnier, Raymond J., Harold G. Halcrow, and Neil H. Jacoby. *Federal Lending and Loan Insurance*, National Bureau of Economic Research. Princeton: Princeton University Press, 1958.

Shull, Bernard. "Changes in Commercial Banking Structure and Small Business Lending." Washington, D.C.: Interagency Task Force on Small Business Finance, December 1981.

Small Business Committee on Capital Access. "Increasing Capital Access for Small Business." Unpublished, October 1982.

Stohl, Hans R. "Small Firms' Access to Public Equity Financing." Washington, D.C.: Interagency Task Force on Small Business Finance, December 1981.

Studenski, Paul, and Herman E. Krooss. *Financial History of the United States: Fiscal, Monetary, Banking, and Tariff, Including Financial Administration and State and Local Finance*. 2nd ed. New York: McGraw-Hill, 1963.

U.S. Congress, General Accounting Office. *SBA's Certified Lenders Program Falls Short of Expectations*. June 1983.

U.S. Congress, General Accounting Office. *SBA's 7(a) Loan Guarantee Program: An Assessment of its Role in the Financial Market*. GAO/RCED–83–96. April 1983.

U.S. Congress, General Accounting Office. *The Small Business Administration Needs to Improve its 7(a) Loan Program*. February 1976.

U.S. Congress. House. Committee on Banking and Currency. *Creation of Small Business Administration*. Hearings. 83rd Cong., 1st sess., May 1953.

U.S. Congress. House. Committee on Small Business. *SBA Legislation and Programs*. Hearings. 97th Cong., 1st sess., March 18, 1981.

U.S. Congress. House. Committee on Small Business. *Summary of Activities*. 97th Cong., 1st sess., December 30, 1982.

U.S. Congress. House. Committee on Small Business. *Impact on Small Business of Proposed Cuts on SBA Guaranteed Loan Program*. Hearings. 97th Cong., 2nd sess., March 31, 1982.

U.S. Congress. House. Committee on Small Business. *SBA Guaranteed Loan Policies*. Hearings. 97th Cong., 1st sess., July 30, 1981.

U.S. Congress. House. Committee on Small Business. *Summary of Activities*. 99th Cong., 2nd sess., H. Rept. 99–1036. January 1987.

U.S. Congress. House. Committee on Small Business. *Financial Assistance Program Termination*. Hearings. 99th Cong., 2nd sess., 1986.

U.S. Congress. House. Committee on Small Business. *1983 Budget Request of the Small Business Administration*. Hearings. 97th Cong., 2nd sess., February 25, 1982.

U.S. Congress. Senate. Committee on Banking and Currency. *Government Lending Agencies*. Hearings. 83rd Cong., 1st sess., May 1953.

U.S. Congress. Senate. Committee on Small Business. *Examination of the Mission of SBA*. Hearings. 96th Cong., 1st sess., October 1979.

U.S. Congress. Senate. Committee on Small Business. *Implementation of Title XVIII of Public Law 99–272, The Reconciliation Act*. Hearings. 100th Cong., 1st sess., 1987.

U.S. Congress. Senate. Committee on Small Business. *Review of the Committee's Activities in the First Session of the 97th Congress*. 97th Cong., 2nd sess., February 1, 1982. Committee Print.

U.S. Congress. Senate. Committee on Small Business. *To Review SBA's Budget Authorization for Fiscal Year 1983*. Hearings. 97th Cong., 2nd sess., February 23, 1982.

U.S. Small Business Administration. *Annual Reports, 1981, 1986*.

U.S. Small Business Administration. "Fact Sheet for Certified Lenders Program and Proposed Preferred Lenders Program." Washington, D.C.: November 1981.

U.S. Small Business Administration. "The Information Book for the SBA Certified Lender Program." Washington, D.C.: 1983. "The Information Book for the Preferred Lender Program." Washington, D.C.: 1984.

U.S. Small Business Administration. Office of Accounting Operations. "Memorandum on Fiscal Year 1982 Loss Rates." Unpublished, March 1983.

U.S. Small Business Administration. *The State of Small Business: A Report of the President*. Washingion, D.C.: GPO, March 1983.

U.S. Treasury Department. *Final Report on the Reconstruction Finance Corporation*. Washington, D.C.: GPO, 1959.

INTERVIEWS

Ball, Bryan, Senior Vice-President, First Georgia Bank, Atlanta, Georgia. By telephone, March 1983.

Barr, Preston, Vice-President, Security Pacific National Bank, Los Angeles, California. By letter, March 1983.

Brown, Greg, SBA Financial Institutions Division. Washington, D.C., 1983 and September 1987.

Chambers, Earl, Director, SBA Office of Portfolio Management. Washington, D.C., September 1984.

Chandler, C. Q., Chairman of the Board, First National Bank in Wichita, Wichita, Kansas. By letter, April 1983.

Chvotkin, Alan, Minority Chief Counsel, Senate Committee on Small Business. Washington, D.C., March 1984.

Clark, Major, Staff Director, House Committee on Small Business. Washington, D.C., March 1984.

Collins, Nathan C., Executive Vice-President, Valley National Bank, Phoenix, Arizona. By letter, May 1983.

Dotchin, Robert, Staff Director, Senate Committee on Small Business. Washington, D.C., March 1983.

Elzey, Tom, Budget Examiner for SBA, Office of Management and Budget. Washington, D.C., 1983.

Estefania, J. Ramon, SBA Actuary. Washington, D.C., 1983.

Garner, C. E., Assistant Vice-President, Bank of America, Los Angeles, California. By letter, March 1983.

Gibb, Dan, SBA Financial Institutions Division. Washington, D.C., 1983.

Gove, Stanley, First Bank Minneapolis, Minneapolis, Minnesota. By telephone, March 1983.

Gurgovits, Steve, Executive Vice-President, First National Bank of Mercer County, Hermitage, Pennsylvania. By telephone, March 1983.

Hammersley, Jim, SBA Financial Institutions Division. Washington, D.C., 1983.

Hertzberg, Charles, SBA Deputy Associate Administrator for Financial Assistance. Washington, D.C., October 1983.

Laforce, Jean, SBA Financial Institutions Division. Washington, D.C., 1983 and September 1987.

Mitchell, Art, Senior Vice-President, Capital Bank and Trust Company, Baton Rouge, Louisiana. By letter, March 1983.

Rosenbaum, Larry, SBA Budget Officer. Washington, D.C., 1982 and 1983.

Sadowski, Chet, Citibank, New York. By telephone, March 1983.

Treptow, Dean, President, Brown Deer Bank, Brown Deer, Wisconsin. By letter, March 1983.

DATA SOURCES

Federal Deposit Insurance Corporation, *Report on Income and Condition*, December 1981. Financial status of banks participating in the SBA program.

Federal Reserve Board, *Bulletin*, various issues, Survey of Terms of Lending at Commercial Banks.

Federal Reserve Board, *Functional Cost Analysis*, various issues.

Robert Morris Associates. *Annual Survey of Commercial Bank Loan Charge-Offs*. Philadelphia, 1980 and 1981.

U.S. Office of Management and Budget, *Budget of the United States Government*, Appendix and Special Analysis on Federal Credit Programs, various years.

U.S. Small Business Administration, Financial Institutions Division. Data on distribution of SBA loans by banks for four states and on performance of certified and preferred lender programs.

U.S. Small Business Administration, Loan Accounting System. All data on histories of individual loans, including size, final disposition, interest rate, and maturity.

U.S. Small Business Administration, "Management Information Survey," October 1984. Status of portfolio.

U.S. Small Business Administration, "7(a) Study as of September 30, 1978." Proportions of loans going to various types of businesses.

Index

Advocacy, as function of SBA, 4, 27, 31
Age of loans, effect on default probability, 37, 42–45, 132
Agent. *See* Principal-agent relationships
Agricultural loans, 141–42
American Bankers Association (ABA), 16, 24, 25, 31
Anderson, Dennis, 96
Appropriations, for SBA loan guarantees, 79, 126–27
Approval time, by SBA of guarantee applications, 3, 112

Banks: advantages over banks in loan making, 80; as agents for SBA (see principal-agent relationships); duties of, under SBA program, 2–3, 39, 77, 99; effect of loan guarantee on, 81–86, 96–97, 105, 124–25, 132; expansion in lending capabilities, 1930s through 1950s, 11–17, 92; influence on SBA program policy, 30–32, 134–35, 138; lending practices, 8, 92–95, 131; quality of SBA loan management by, 7–8, 38, 77; rates of return received for SBA loans, 7–8, 52, 55–61, 86–87; and the second-ary market in SBA loans, 115–22; strategies for participation in SBA program, 3, 56–57, 61–69; as suppliers of term loans, 19, 22, 45, 90, 92, 132; support for SBA program, 1, 16, 18, 20–21, 24–26; types of, participating in SBA program, 69–75. *See also* Certified lender program; Preferred lender program

Bates, Timothy, 4–5
Beneficiaries: of credit programs generally, 137–38, 141, 143–44; defaults among, 84; of SBA loan guarantee program, 8, 20–24, 55, 79; social and economic contributions of, 90. *See also* Constituency; Interest Groups
Benefits of SBA loan guarantee program: to banks, 69, 74–75, 112, 116–17; to Congressional supporters, 26–28; social and economic, 5–6, 8, 35, 89–91, 97–108
Birch, David, 98
Bond markets, 13, 92–93, 120–21
Bonds, corporate, 13, 59
Borrowers. *See* Beneficiaries
Brokers who trade in SBA guaranteed loans, 25, 30, 116
Budget, U.S., 26; budgetary treatment

About the Author

ELISABETH HOLMES RHYNE is a consultant specializing in international development. The research for the present work was conducted with the help and cooperation of the Brookings Institution and the Congressional Budget Office.